östberg™

Library of Design Management

"Jim Cramer's book is about leadership and action and is full of fresh ideas. It offers hope that things can get better. This book is right on target for design professionals preparing for the future. It is a personal and rich weave not only useful but also indispensable.
I think you'll enjoy it"

MAX DUPREE, HON. AIA
CHAIRMAN EMERITUS, HERMAN MILLER COMPANY AND
AUTHOR, *LEADERSHIP IS AN ART* AND *LEADERSHIP JAZZ*

"Jim Cramer's exceptional book is about architects and clients and better ways to satisfy both. Architecture designed for human use... exceeds the expectations of each in an emerging new reality. This book should be relevant for many years to come."

JONAS SALK, M.D.

"Jim Cramer has produced an outstanding anthology for and about the future of architecture and architects. It paints a welcome and convincing portrait of the opportunity Society is asking today's architects to grasp, and makes clear there are leadership strategies that architects can adopt to make it all happen."

WELD COXE
EMERITUS FOUNDING PRINCIPAL, THE COXE GROUP INC.

"This book points out that success in the design field rests upon the relationships of trust and loyalty that are established by the designer's effort and the client's needs and interests. I appreciate the message of identifying new opportunities and the many creative ways to take advantage of them."

GERALD S. HOBBS
CHAIRMAN AND CEO, VNU NORTH AMERICA

"Jim Cramer sees successful architects as playing on a worldwide stage, offering creative relevance and value, not just as spear carriers, but full leaders in every sense of the word including—horror of horrors—assuming risk inherent in true leadership of the building team."
HAROLD ADAMS, FAIA
CHAIRMAN, RTKL INTERNATIONAL, INC.

DESIGN

plus

ENTERPRISE

SEEKING A NEW REALITY
IN ARCHITECTURE & DESIGN

J A M E S   P .   C R A M E R

DESIGN

plus

ENTERPRISE

SEEKING A NEW REALITY
IN ARCHITECTURE & DESIGN

UPDATED AND EXPANDED EDITION

GreenwayConsulting   **östberg**

First published by The American Institute of Architects Press

LCCN: 2001098416

ISBN: 0-9675477-3-3

Östberg Library of Design Management

Greenway Communications, LLC

a division of The Greenway Group

30 Technology Parkway South, Suite 200

Norcross, GA 30309

(800) 726-8603

www.greenwayconsulting.com

Distributed in North America by

National Book Network

(800) 462-6420

www.nbnbooks.com

To Carol B. Cramer
and to Mentorship

To Jonas Salk
and to Imaginative Research

To George White
and to Leadership

To Bill Caudill
and to Talking Action

CONTENTS

EMBRACING CHANGE

THE SUCCESSFUL FIRM

TOWARD PERSONAL FULFILLMENT

THE ASCENDENT DESIGNER

ADDITIONAL RESOURCES

ACKNOWLEDGEMENTS

FOREWORD

HAROLD L. ADAMS, FAIA, RIBA, JIA

F ew of us are granted the opportunity to view architecture globally, and to view it in the perspective of time as the practice moves worldwide and reflects worldwide cycles of triumph and adversity. Jim Cramer has had this opportunity. And he took full advantage of it.

In his book *Design plus Enterprise*, he shares with us his wide-ranging observations and his keen insights, which are on the one hand global and on the other hand local. He has experienced the greatest building boom in the past one hundred years as well as the greatest building depression in this century. What lessons could be learned; what morals could be drawn? What is the meaning of it all to the average practitioner?

This is the focus of Jim's book—what it all means to you, to me, and to our fellow architects. What emerges as a driving dominant theme is a call for design leadership in the broadest sense of that word—leadership by the architect of not just design but all aspects of the total team effort.

Jim redefines and broadens the word "design" to embrace not just conceptual graphic skill, but also business and technical competence.

Jim sees successful architects as playing on a worldwide stage, offering creative relevance and value, not just as spear carriers, but full leaders, including—horror of horrors—assuming the risk inherent in true leadership of the building team. He defines his total leadership as essential to success in today's terms, and concludes that never have the opportunities for the profession been greater.

The book's subtitle, *Seeking A New Reality in Architecture & Design*, reinforces Jim's theme and sharpens its focus. Every chapter is filled with common sense observations, with relevant suggestions, and is illustrated with examples drawn from real life.

This book offers a rich and diverse agenda of great value to all practitioners, large and small.

INTRODUCTION

RAYMOND P. RHINEHART, PH.D., HON. AIA

We live in an artificial world. All animals shape their environment to suit their needs, but none on the scale of the human animal. We may think local; our impact, however, is global. Indeed, we have become co-equals with nature in determining how this planet evolves.

Making the right or appropriate choices as we shape the world around us would seem to be a matter of common sense as much as enlightened self-interest.

But as we walk the streets of our dangerous cities or inch along the highways of clogged suburban sprawl, the evidence of our eyes argues common sense is neither. Too often we allocate our resources and manipulate the countryside like rank amateurs, guided solely by convenience and profit. No other animal would either intentionally or by accident shape a nest, hollow, or burrow guaranteed to fail. We do it all the time.

Design plus Enterprise is about making the right choices. As such, it is dedicated to professionals, *design* professionals. The author assumes (I believe correctly) that as a species, designers have the innate gifts and training to guide their immediate clients (those who pay the bills) and their ultimate clients (the public) to make decisions that help steer this planet toward a better future. Jim Cramer likes, is genuinely fascinated by, and is fiercely committed to the men and women he views as an indispensable resource in this great evolutionary journey.

There is much to argue that designers *and* their clients are up to the task. Individual buildings at every scale and even whole communities show it is possible to juggle skillfully form, commodity, and delight. But the very fact that we travel to these sites on our vacations or, at the very least, make them subjects of design awards programs indicates they are somewhat out of the ordinary. The effort might be compared to a trip to a museum or zoo to see some exotic phenomenon behind bars or in a hermetically sealed glass case.

If designers have the creativity and training, and if we, the public, certainly have the need, where is the breakdown? What goes wrong?

Like a coach, Jim Cramer argues that success has as much to do with a positive, winning attitude as it does with any residual strength. A winning attitude is the adrenaline that pumps up and powers our creative muscles. It bridges the distance between idea and action. Preparing for success is as integral to succeeding as a laissez faire attitude or outright pessimism is to failure.

A winning attitude is not easy. It's not the equivalent of pinning a happy face on the captain of the Titanic. A winning attitude takes a lot of hard, honest work. It begins with an assumption that we do have a choice, we can make a difference among others and within ourselves. That's the first, biggest, and most important step. After that, a winning attitude requires close scrutiny of the world that puts a premium on facts. It means developing the fine art of *active* listening. It steers clear of passivity, but understands the crucial difference between aggression and assertiveness.

A winning attitude is magnanimous, people oriented, and involved because it is caring. It values a kind of leadership that does not bully but, rather, empowers and enables. A winning attitude does not avoid, it celebrates change. It embraces not only the new opportunities uncovered by change, but also thrives on the climate of energy generated by every stretching of the envelope. This trait alone would identify design professionals as a resource uniquely positioned to address some of the most intractable problems of our time. As Jim Cramer writes: "The public sees architects as innovators, problem solvers, and among the most fascinating professionals in the world. That makes them valuable to all the rest of us non-architects who are also trying to negotiate the twists and turns of the emerging new world."

> " *A winning attitude is magnanimous, people oriented, and involved because it is caring.* "

In Jim Cramer's lexicon of winning strategies, "business" is not a dirty word. Doing business is not the price or compromise of what it means to be a professional designer; it is the ticket to the main event of shaping a better world. In this light, knowing how to negotiate effectively is not a distraction. It combines many of the points raised a moment ago, such as the art of listening. But it also includes a clear-eyed appreciation of the designer's own worth, which is not a bad piece of knowledge to have at any time. Here's what Cramer has to say on the subject: "Vision, a commitment to growth and planning, a real familiarity with writing and speaking skills, a 'can do' approach to any problem—they're all part of the negotiator's art. But they're also the vital signs of a well-run practice and a profession posed to harness the energy of change to power future success."

Design plus Enterprise is colored by the kind of enthusiasm for design professionals that only a design nonprofessional could have without any embarrassment. Never complacent in its admiration, it urges these extraordinary individuals who have so much to offer to our lives to train with the intensity of an athlete going for the gold. To run the race in this manner, Cramer insists, is to make winners of us all.

THE DESIGN PLUS ENTERPRISE MODEL

JAMES P. CRAMER

I wasn't always fascinated with architecture and design. I'm not an architect, but I have come to realize how important good design is as an ingredient to better human health and well being. And how important business skills are to successful practice.

Design is not as well understood as we would like it to be. It's quite common to encounter people who say that design is a waste of time and money. Nevertheless, with each passing month, it becomes more apparent to me that good design is not only advisable but crucial to both competitive advantage and a better quality of life. Good design is a key to ensuring economic viability and business leadership. Indeed, good design is good business.

> **Successful firms see trends and then get ahead of them.**

Design, however, needs more advocates. More soul mates. More sellers and persuaders. Good design needs leaders who are positioned to be listened to and who can deliver the message with clarity and conviction.

In a recent presentation of the Presidential Design Awards, eight benefits of good design were offered:

1. Good design can improve the quality of our lives.
2. Good design can enhance American competitiveness.

3. Good design can save time and money.
4. Good design can improve performance.
5. Good design can simplify use, manufacture, and maintenance.
6. Good design can improve safety.
7. Good design can enhance communications.
8. Good design can preserve historic and natural resources.

I come from experiences where I see good design not as a luxury but as a necessity. However, the delivery systems for good design are currently far too weak. There is much to be done. This book is about my research leading to a new understanding not only about the importance of good design but about the positioning and principles necessary for success. For I believe there is a map of expanding opportunity for architects and new competitive advantages through design.

This book is about change—a new model, if you will, leading toward an expanding definition for the profession of architecture.

Churchill said, "success is never final." Success is a journey. The only problem with being a success is that you have to keep on being a success. Successful people aren't just lucky. Good things happen because people are willing to think smart, work hard, take risks, and be resilient.

Not long ago I spoke to the students and faculty at the Massachusetts Institute of Technology during their spring lecture series. During the presentation, I said the choices we make put us on a pathway. By Sunday night we are not the same person we were at the beginning of the week. Week after week, if we learn well, we will get better, stronger, and be of more value—not just in school or our career but especially to our family, friends, and, yes, to ourselves.

With self-esteem, which is to say the value you place on yourself, comes an ability to be resilient and uncommonly optimistic, seeing opportunity where others see only a mass of problems.

Dr. Jonas Salk says, "where there's a will, there's a way. Unfortunately, where there's a way, there's not always a will." We need designers, architects, clients, and political leaders of will and courage to find a new way. The most important intellectual breakthrough of our time is the realization that nothing is impossible. However, we shall not achieve great goals with limited vision. We shall not achieve relevant and satisfying professional careers with petty services. We will not find our way guided only by small dreams. Choice, not chance, determines destiny.

This book is about pathways and dreams. It is about real life success stories. A Sunday *New York Times* article headline from the 1990s reads "Efficiency, Not Ego, Gives Edge to Designer." The article is about M. Arthur Gensler, Jr., a San Francisco-based architect. The point being made is that at a time when more companies are rethinking the amount of office space they need, the Gensler firm continues to grow. Why? Because this firm makes its clients' needs the top priority. The firm is noted for listening and then delivering full value. So what happened to Gensler? In the year following the article, billings rose 6 percent and the firm opened six new offices. [Since then, the firm has

4 grown to more than 2000 employees and become a benchmark for quality design and business resiliency. In 2000, Gensler won the AIA Firm of the Year Award, one of the industry's highest honors.]

Like Gensler, there are many firms that are successful because they see trends and get ahead of them. They continually listen and develop a dialogue of empathy with the business community. This book will take a closer look at these firms and what they are doing to keep themselves competitive.

> *Architects and designers will be at the center of relevancy and value.*

I have traveled exhaustively across America and much of Europe and Asia. I have talked with hundreds of people in the construction, business, and design communities. Some feel that the architectural profession is headed in the wrong direction and slipping into decline. But they are not representative of those who consistently realize success. These architects and their supportive, insightful clients have persuaded me to remain optimistic about the strength and value of the profession. To them the current turmoil is not a sign of decline, but the opportunity to create a new identity and with it a new reality.

In the future I see architects at the center of relevancy and value. Not just players but leaders. Not just offering traditional services, but offering creative full services. Not just coordinating, but collaborating.

Not just marginally rewarded, but fully compensated. Not just concerned about design and quality, but with courageous insight and economic relevance offering inspiration during negotiations.

This much I know based on stories of progress from all over the globe: As concern grows for shaping a better, more compassionate world, we are entering an era of great opportunity for the enterprising architect. For many, it will be a new and deeply fulfilling reality.

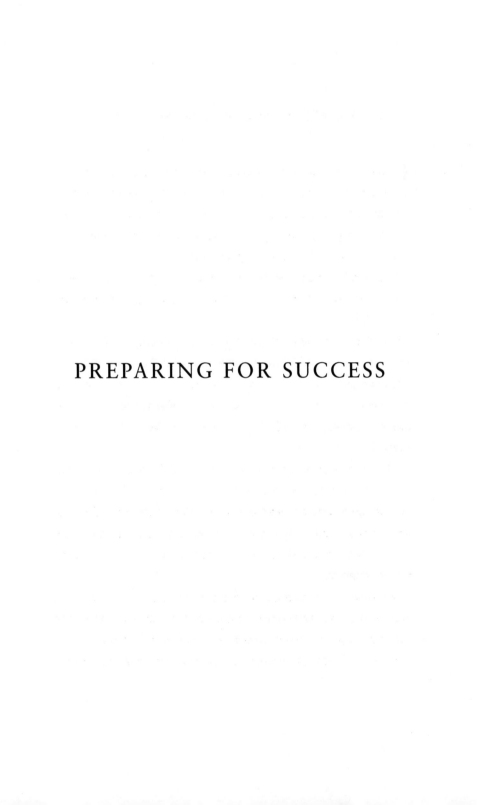

PREPARING FOR SUCCESS

SIR NORMAN FOSTER, RIBA, HON. FAIA

I have always believed passionately that architecture is a social art—a necessity and not a luxury—that it is concerned with the quality of life—the creation of benefits—about caring and sharing. Social concern is one of the most powerful driving forces of architecture.

The credits start with the most important people—the prime movers—those progressive clients who commission the buildings.

It is they who establish goals and set standards by their foresight and courage. Without inspired leadership from individuals, politicians, and institutions, there is little that we can achieve for society as a whole. I would like to pay tribute to the exceptional individuals that we have been privileged to work for.

The architect is traditionally responsible for design. But design is not a fashionable "ism"—it is about people and borne out of the needs of people. It is easy to forget that the pioneers of modern architecture were essentially concerned with social conditions and sought to raise standards in the home and workplace.

Architecture is also about the spiritual needs of people as well as their material needs. It has much to do with optimism, joy, and reassurance—of order in a disordered world—of privacy in the midst of many, of space in a crowded site, of light in a dull day. It is about quality—the quality of the space and the poetry of the light that models it.

Then there is the more private world within our buildings. A vital part of the architect's job is to respect and listen to the users-to bring their voices forward as a positive influence-because it is they who will be living with the end result.

There is much scope, even in a single building, for the architect to work directly with industry; to be involved in the design of the products, which come together to make the building; to create a spirit of loving care so that no detail is considered too small; and to channel the pride of a work force into a job well done. Quality and satisfaction are far more likely to come from closer links between those who design and those who make. That isn't a fashionable line today, but if I ran a school of architecture, that would be my manifesto.

We must learn from the failure and successes of the past. To respond to the challenge of tackling the difficult deprived areas and resisting the easier pickings of fringe suburbia. To rediscover the culture of mixed-use. The integration of new, cleaner industries into neighborhoods. To seek the potential of greener, more ecologically sensitive structures. To harness the economy and poetry of renewable energies—where the sun would be a friend and not an enemy.

OPTIMISM IS THE PARENT OF SUCCESS

"I am an optimist.
It does not seem too much use being anything else."

MICHEL DE MONTAIGNE

A principal of a large firm stopped by my office. He was in Washington on business and had decided on the spur of the moment to drop in to ask a single question: "Jim, are you optimistic about the profession's future?" Somewhat taken aback by his directness, I responded, "Why, yes, I am, for many reasons!" He shot back, "I'm happy you said that. We're paying over $50,000 a year in dues to the AIA and I need to know it's a good investment." With that, he got up and went about his other business.

I know of few leaders in the design profession who are not optimistic. The key word here is "leaders." Defeatism is not a property of leadership. It rolls off the back of a leader like water off a duck. Defeatism is a self-fulfilling autopsy. I think failure, therefore I am.

President Lincoln once said, "The pessimist sees the difficulty in every opportunity and the optimist sees the opportunity in every difficulty." As much by the force of his personality as his armies with their rotating generals, Lincoln went on to win what others said was a hopeless war.

I believe successful designers are those who truly enjoy the challenge of creativity, innovation, and problem solving. Design leaders bring health to every situation. Their optimism—firmly rooted in a clear-eyed, honest appreciation of their own gifts—is infectious. It energizes the design team.

Clients are especially susceptible to and grateful for this kind of energy. They value candid, upbeat designers, who they hire to *solve*, not invent, problems. With this kind of leadership, the design enterprise prospers.

Accentuating the positive does not inevitably lead to success. Designers can't control every element of the dynamic, vastly complex process that is design.

> *Design leaders bring health to every situation.*

Even Lincoln had his Bull Runs. But designers can control the kind of energy and enthusiasm they bring to a project.

Who is better prepared for the future: those who look over their shoulders at real or imagined shadows or those who protect their rear flank by boldly embracing the future?

MEASURING UP

"People who get ahead are those who prove
they can get things done."

DAVID KEARNS

What does it take to be admired? An act of statesmanship or artistic breakthrough qualifies. Ministers and rabbis who provide moral and ethical leadership are among the most admired in their communities. So are Nobel Prize winners, CNN reporters under fire, astronauts, and Notre Dame head coaches.

Among America's architects, H.H. Richardson and Frank Lloyd Wright head up the list of most admired, as do the living AIA Gold Medallists, Pritzker Prize winners, Herman Miller chairman emeritus Max DePree, and practitioners like architects Leonard Parker and Cesar Pelli, who demonstrate that it's possible to design public buildings and campus facilities that beat budgets, respect the dignity of the users, and celebrate good design.

Admiration doesn't require much acreage to flourish. How many of us had our lives changed thanks to a patient teacher who took some extra time to find something in us that even our parents didn't see?

Building on reputation

Whatever line of work we're in, reputation is the bedrock on which admiration is built. What goes into solidifying that rock? A piece published recently in *Fortune* magazine identified what its editors called the "eight key attributes of reputation":

1. Quality of management
2. Quality of products or services
3. Innovativeness
4. Long-term investment value
5. Financial soundness
6. Ability to attract, develop, and keep talented people
7. Community and environmental responsibility
8. Wise use of corporate assets

Where do you stand?

If your professional practice and business peers-both in and outside the construction industry-were ranking you, where would you stand on a scale of 0 (bottom of the barrel) to 10 (candidate for sainthood)? Just as important, in which direction would you be perceived to be moving?

> **In which direction are you perceived to be moving?**

The annual *Fortune* survey of America's top businesses is a useful reminder of two things: First, the value of reputation and, second, that reputation is a dynamic currency constantly changing in value depending on the decisions we make. Once lost or compromised, it's difficult to restore; firmly in place, it's one of the most persuasive arguments we bring to the bargaining table.

ETHICS: BRIDGE OVER TROUBLED WATERS

"Ethics and leadership always join in behavior. Our voices, our words, are essential but in vain without action."

MAX DEPREE

As most architects have discovered, public recognition for one's best shot isn't inevitable. We can't depend on applause from others. Instead, we must be our own cheering section, especially when times are tough.

Yes, we can look to positive role models for guidance and seek the advice of trusted friends. These are invaluable back ups, but only back ups. They can't take the place of a steady moral compass.

In the end, we've got to reach deep inside ourselves to do what's right, sometimes with no more coaching than the voice inside us. That's hard enough when work is rolling in. But in a tough economy, keeping a steady eye on our moral compass is a very lonely vigil, especially if one's survival is at stake.

Tough times call for tough decisions

A measure of the strain comes from reports that document a rise in cases involving professional ethics. The strain is understandable. But our personal code of ethics, our ability to put right actions before mere expediency-this is of greatest value *precisely* when decisions are toughest to make. Ethical conduct is not an option in bad weather; it's the one indispensable resource likely to steer us safely into better times. Our ability to hold on to fortune and even friends is never absolute. But a mind at peace with itself cannot be assailed by the worst life throws at us.

SURVIVAL OF THE WISEST

"Man can learn wisdom from nature...[A]lthough we cannot predict the future, with understanding Man can, to a considerable degree, influence the course of coming events in his favor. Man's past performance should not be taken as the only basis for judging his future."

JONAS SALK, M.D.

Several lessons can be drawn from the familiar story about the blind men who are asked to describe an elephant. One that appeals to me is the useful knowledge that for many problems or challenges there is often more than one right answer.

But to hear some architects talk, there is only one way of doing things—their way. I wonder if they haven't grabbed their elephant at the wrong end.

In his *Ascent of Man*, Jacob Bronowski writes about the impossibility of positively knowing the right answer no matter the question: "There is not absolute knowledge, and those who claim it—whether they are scientists or dogmatists—open the door to tragedy. All information is imperfect. We have to treat it with humility."

Bronowski's point is well taken; it's as old as history itself. Nearly 2,500 years ago, the oracle at Delphi tapped Socrates as the wisest human being because he was the only mortal smart enough to admit he knew nothing for certain. His was the wisdom of humility.

Hindsight is a great ally of humility. When I was publisher of *Architectural Technology* and group publisher of *Architecture*, I remember how hard we pursued excellence. We wouldn't start the presses until we were convinced we had gotten the magazine right. Weeks later when the printed copies landed on my desk, the warts and blemishes would almost always still be found. They'd fairly jump out! How could we have missed them?

Hindsight and humility will help an architect listen more closely to his or her clients. Both the hindsight and humility give us permission to entertain the liberating thought that there may be several ways to achieve a desired end-different but equally right.

> *Hindsight and humility will help an architect listen more closely to clients.*

One thing more: armed with hindsight and humility, we will be more prepared to face our inevitable shortcomings and more open to do a better job the next time around.

An open mind begets wisdom. The architect possessing wisdom is what the marketplace is looking for. The late Dr. Jonas Salk talked of this as "survival of the wisest." This is a powerful message to a profession in transition.

SURVIVING THE WINTER OF YOUR DISCONTENT

"Planning for your future is important. It is where you will
spend the rest of your life."

DAVID CASTRO-BLANCO, FAIA

A *Wall Street Journal* article began, "Damn the torpor, full speed ahead…" The inspired juggling of a familiar quotation caught my mood as I thought about the dismal economy of the year just ended and the challenges ahead.

Construction—as we're told over and over again—is a cyclical industry: Inevitable downdrafts are just as inevitably followed by rebounds. The trick is to look beyond the present and set a course for the future.

The message? Slack times are opportunities to get your house in order and plan for growth in the long term. Here's a to-do list when the wolf is howling outside your door:

1. **Let the future, not the present, define your horizons.** Design the future you want then work toward achieving your goal.

2. **Make an inventory of resources.** There is more out there than you think-networking with your colleagues, community contacts, the growing number of electronic services, programs offered by your professional association-and that's just for openers.

3. Use down time to pursue professional development. New skills and services will give you a competitive edge. Take a public speaking or writing course. In the information age, it pays to be a good communicator.

4. Work for a more favorable legislative and regulatory environment. Get involved in the political process.

5. Support the development of a national design literacy. Let's face it: there's often a big gap between the value we confidently know good design brings to any human activity and the appreciation of that value by the very clients and the public that designers seek to serve.

In other words, when the skies are most threatening, it often pays to keep your eye on where you want to go, not where you are. The only way to get on the other side of the present difficulty is to set your course for a better future and then open the throttle, full speed ahead.

THE TRANSFORMATIONAL POWER OF DESIGN

"Design is an essential component of our society. It affects the structure of our homes, the ways we travel and communicate, and the ways we conduct our business. At its best, design can beautify our cities, encourage economic development and social change, and profoundly affect our lives...[D]esigners help to ensure our nation's competitiveness and reputation for quality of generations to come."

PRESIDENTIAL DESIGN AWARDS

A few years back, a small but powerful show was mounted at Washington's National Gallery of Art. Called "The Greek Miracle," the exhibition highlighted thirty-four pieces of fifth-century classical sculpture. I recall standing still for some time in front of a fragment of the Parthenon frieze showing charging cavalry. Yes, it was thrilling. I could almost hear the thunder of the horses' hoofs and see their marble flanks sweat.

But "miraculous," as the title of the exhibition insisted? For all the beauty of this exhibition, nothing seemed really that miraculous or out of the ordinary to my eye. Then it hit me—*that* was the miracle. As soon as I had walked into the gallery, I felt right at home. My eye responded to and easily understood a design vocabulary first spoken twenty-five centuries ago.

But imagine the response of a visitor to fifth-century Athens. The sights were nothing like what would have been encountered anywhere else in the known world. The effect on those who first saw what we've come to call the "classical ideal" must have hovered nervously someplace between exhilaration and shock. No doubt traditionalists found the Acropolis puzzling, if not offensive.

The real miracle is that in less than a couple of generations, the architects and artists of a small Greek city-state set the future course of Western art. Surely their greatest achievement was to transform how we regard ourselves and the world around us. What had been revolutionary in their time became the common ideal against which everything since has been measured.

A *new way of seeing*

In a similar way, Frank Lloyd Wright created a way of looking at modern architecture. That's what imagination, creativity, and genius do in any age—they bring miracles down to earth.

Look at early photos of Frank Lloyd Wright's work in and around Oak Park. We've all seen them. What's curious or odd in those photographs? To most viewers it's not Wright's architecture, which we could imagine living in quite nicely. No, it's the Queen Anne-style houses and the Model T Fords. They belong to another, distant time. Yet they came *after* Wright's first important Oak Park commissions. Try to imagine how the Unity Temple struck contemporary passersby when it was newly built. It must have looked as alien as the Starship *Enterprise*.

Wright's architecture no longer astonishes because Wright made his particular design insights part of our common visual vocabulary. Architecture has not been the same.

Architects see into how things should be

Our times call for miracles as we try to be better stewards of our greatest resource—the planet on which more and more human beings dwell. The times call for a fundamental shift in the way we shelter human enterprise. Who is in a better position to transform the unusual, the extraordinary, the miraculous into standard practice if not the architect working with planners, other design professionals, contractors, manufacturers, public officials, and, most important, the public?

This generation is challenged to set the stage for what could, in the hindsight of future historians, be one of the most radical leaps forward of our civilization. If today's architects meet this challenge, the inheritance of our children will be more livable places.

Today such places are minor miracles. If we succeed, they will be tomorrow's commonplaces.

"I can't imagine a person becoming a success who doesn't give this game of life everything he's got."

WALTER CRONKITE

Architects don't have to look far for answers. A lot of what the profession needs to succeed can be picked up by looking at architects who even in a restructuring of the profession find real satisfaction in their work.

Of course, job satisfaction is a highly subjective matter. But from what I've seen, those who find satisfaction in their work observe most if not all of the following:

[handwritten: — professional dev.]

1. **They have a commitment to self-improvement.** Successful professionals constantly hone their craft. If architects are going to speak the language of increasingly sophisticated clients, they need to be familiar with emerging information technologies and pursue new business skills eagerly.

2. **They do not knock their colleagues.** Why do so many architects spend energy tearing each other down? The level of the profession isn't raised in the public's eye by beating up on one's colleagues. Infighting gives competing forces outside the profession a competitive edge. Total market share is reduced.

3. **They welcome change.** One of the few things we know about the future with any certainty is that it's going to

be different. Those who are prepared will welcome the new opportunities change inevitably brings. The rest will be forced to scramble just to survive.

4. **They don't whine.** Some architects complain the public doesn't understand or value their services. Recently, I attended a gathering of clients and media representatives who were listening to a local leader of the profession. What we all heard was a depressing litany of the ways in which architects were not being appreciated. Without denying the real challenges facing the profession in a rapidly changing world, the fact remains that the primary responsibility for being valued falls squarely on your shoulders. Put yourself in the shoes of potential clients: what must they be thinking when they hear architects ask for their pity rather than their confidence?

5. **They seek out opportunities to exercise leadership.** Leadership is present in classrooms where architects work with young children; it happens in the office of a client who is persuaded to invest in an environmentally sound project; it's heard at town meetings where citizen architects lead their neighbors in informed discussions about land use and quality, affordable housing. Leadership lifts the eyes of the clients and the public alike from mere expediency out to the horizon and beyond. Weld Coxe puts it this way: "The leader defines reality."

6. **They listen but are not passive.** Being a good listener is critical to teamwork and the ultimate quality of the most public of the arts. But successful architects are

not satisfied with being sympathetic ears; as design experts they must lead the dialogue. That doesn't mean being a bully; it does mean being gifted in the art of persuasion. Real success begins with a thorough, sympathetic understanding of a client's needs.

And now comes the fine print:

Being a good critical listener—along with a commitment to leadership and lifelong learning, a positive attitude (which includes being supportive of one another), and an openness to change—is what all successful, profoundly rewarding careers have in common. Putting it more simply: Success is the moral equivalent of believing in your profession and in yourself.

THE DESIGNER IS SYNERGISTIC

"Make not little plans; they have no magic to stir men's blood and probably themselves will not be realized. Make big plans; aim high in hope and work, remembering that a noble, logical diagram, once recorded, will not die."

DANIEL BURNHAM

S ome physicists argue the universe is running down. Their word for it is entropy. I prefer to place my bets on an opposing phenomenon—synergy.

People are synergistic who improve almost any situation they get into. They understand what is happening around them. They bring health. They work smart. They are innovative as they involve people around them in exploring new ways of thinking and doing.

A sublimely gifted but modest architect from Arkansas won the AIA Gold Medal in 1990. Fay Jones received this honor in a special White House cere-

> *The power of synergy animates the entire team.*

mony. Later that same day, Prince Charles of Great Britain gave him a fine tribute in the soaring space of the National Building Museum before a large audience of government officials, corporate leaders, and design superstars. The applause was as much for the man as the inspired creator of such twentieth-century masterpieces as Thorncrown Chapel.

I've been privileged to gain an insight into how Fay Jones works. When he negotiates and communicates with others in seemingly adversarial situations, he separates the people from the problem. He helps others to be right. He focuses on their interests and concerns and does not fight over his own preconceptions.

Gradually, others understand his innovative and creative problem-coaxing process. Instead of frustration and confrontation, synergistic solutions bubble to the surface. The resulting ideas are often much better than the original concept. There is creativity, not compromise. Mediocrity is not on the range of considerations. The power released by synergy animates the entire team, bringing forth new solutions and wonderful results.

In the way he works, Fay Jones is not a phenomenon but a type. He belongs to that happy tribe of warriors who conquer others not by the force of their ego, but by their skill in enlisting others in the joy of a shared enterprise.

TRAINING FOR THE GOLD

"If ambition doesn't hurt you, you haven't got it."

KATHLEEN NORRIS

P ractice fitness. Convey to others that you are a top performer. Once when I served as a designer selection consultant to a Fortune 100 corporation, the architect who had entered the interview as the leading candidate was in the end not selected. There was no question about the designer's credentials. They were impeccable. Indeed, everything on paper said this was the firm for the job. But the interview went wrong in a subtle though profound way. The architect came across as tired, not really up to the rigors of a $60 million capital project. The selection committee was competitive and performance-oriented. They wanted the same of their lead architect.

There was little said about the architect's lack of energy during the final review of candidate firms, but make no mistake: it was the decisive factor between the winner and the loser. The references were there; the portfolio was dazzling. But there was no fire, no foot halfway over the starting line eager to sprint down the track toward success.

> *Stamina and energy have a lot to do with swaying the selection process*

How often has a job been lost after weeks of the most painstaking preparations because the would-be client sees a designer who doesn't seem to have the spark to go for the gold?

The perception clients have of a design professional's stamina and energy have a lot more to do with swaying the selection process than most would admit. The playing field is no place to be caught napping.

Stay fit and take care of yourself. Conduct yourself like a champion. Never lose the fire that reassures a client you won't settle for anything less than success.

"need fire in the belly"

THE BEGINNING OF A BEAUTIFUL RELATIONSHIP

"The provision of an inspiring background is not a misplaced bit of romanticism; it is the architect's life work."

CHARLES W. MOORE, FAIA

The entrance to architect John Carl Warnecke's New York home has a gallery showing three generations of architectural drawings, including those of his father and his daughter. Wherever your eye rests, the family's sensitivity to the art of architecture is handsomely displayed.

This enthusiasm for his craft shows through in Warnecke's work. He is an artist with a human touch. Or, as George White, former Architect of the U.S. Capitol, said:

Architects are often admired and respected for different reasons, including their design talents or their professionalism or their business acumen or their magnetism or their personality. Jack Warnecke is one of the individuals with whom I have been privileged to work who gains admiration, respect, and affection in full and equal measure. I believe that his architecture achieves lasting qualities not only because of his skillful use of form and materials, but also because of the warm, inviting spirit that permeates his work.

Warnecke is the architect of the state capitol in Hawaii,

as well as Washington's Hart Senate Office Building and,
on the other side of town, the New Executive Office
Building, which handsomely complements Lafayette
Square. From the perspective of his retirement, he can look
back at having run one of the largest and most influential
firms in the United States. What is not so well known,
however, is his skill in cultivating long-term relationships
with his clients. Even in his retirement, he is routinely
called upon to consult on efficient maintenance, remodeling options, additions, and improvements of projects that
were built many years ago.

People matter to this architect. He enjoys being of value
to them. He has both a genuine interest and the discipline
to follow up with clients on matters
important to them: cards during the hol-
idays, phone calls of congratulations on
anniversaries or birthdays, remembering
names of family members. What all this
special attention adds up to in the eyes of
the client is, "This architect is my
friend—he cares!"

*Architecture
achieves lasting
qualities because
of the warm,
inviting spirit.*

Warnecke is a tough act to follow, but the basis of his
success is available to any architect and designer:

- **Be enthusiastic.** You must be passionate about your
  work and your profession to succeed.
- **Make the case for quality.** Quality increases the use-
  fulness of a building and diminishes the future costs of
  its maintenance and inevitable renovation. A project is
  a long-term commitment: don't make it a burden.

quality
vs
value.

- **The heart of successful client relationships is attention to details.** Client relationships never end with the completion of a project. Carefully cultivated, they will deepen over a lifetime and will, in many instances, bring future commissions.

YOUR IMAGE AND YOUR CLIENT'S EXPECTATIONS

"You can be the best designer. But unless your communication skills meet the client's expectations, your design skills won't get you anywhere."

SYLVESTER DAMIANOS, FAIA

A re you an advocate for your own success? Clients need reassurances. Is their confidence in you well placed? They look for this reassurance each time they come in contact with you.

What you say, how you say it, how you look, and what you value positions you for leadership. Does the message you broadcast communicate creativity, quality, and design excellence?

Communication is not merely the words we speak, although I don't want to understate the crucial importance of speaking clearly. But we do send other signals as well. Most of us have heard the phrase "walk the walk, talk the talk." Unless we identify ourselves as the walking, talking spokespersons for design and leadership, the message loses power; it might not even get through.

First impressions count

Communications expert Dr. Roger Flax says that people form their strongest impressions of us in the first minute of an initial encounter. What we say after that simply confirms that initial impression, which, if it's way off base, is difficult to overcome or erase. Knowing that is both a challenge and an opportunity.

There's a story about a college student who was about to be interviewed for a prestigious fellowship. He was one of a half dozen finalists, all of whom sat together in the parlor of a New York brownstone, nervously waiting their turn to be questioned by an intimidating panel.

When the pocket doors were pulled back and he was called to come into the interview, he got up from his chair and walked to the opening. As he entered the next room, the toe of his shoe caught the edge of the carpet and he fell headfirst at the feet of the startled panel. From that position, he looked up at the concerned faces and, without blinking an eye, said, "Well, at least I've fallen into good company." The panel had found its winning candidate.

> **The image we project will determine the number of opportunities for success.**

In this world, there are no automatic winners. But let there be no doubt: the image we project will largely determine the number of opportunities we will have to be successful.

Watch how the pros do it

I've learned a lot about winning first impressions by the way top flight designers such as Gene Kohn, Hugh Hardy, and Massimo Vignelli walk into a room. Watch Gold Medallist Sir Norman Foster, former University of Texas at Austin Dean Hal Box, and Minnesota architects James

Stageberg and Bill Beyer. Each, in his own way, has almost instant rapport with individuals they've just met or with a large audience in a crowded hall.

Look into the mirror and deep into yourself: an honest assessment of the image you project can provide valuable insights. How strong and how positive is the message that stares back at you?

Accentuate the best in yourself. The figure you cut— your composite message about your values and what it is that makes good design worth advocating—will fall into good company.

A CALL TO SERVICE

THE HONORABLE RICHARD SWETT, FAIA

In architecture, buildings are designed not only as aesthetic sculptures but as functional structures that serve their inhabitants. The key is to combine the two in such a way as to provide for both the pragmatic and inspirational needs of the users. The debate and discussion in this process reflect mutual respect and most importantly a desire by all the parties to find an agreement. This is really the approach that is built upon a win-win foundation.

Take the simple design of a house. The client is not one person, but the entire family. Each person has preferences that are different from others. The different preferences, by human nature, inflate or deflate certain aspects of the house in the eye of the individual. Those who like to cook want large kitchens, people prone to throw big social events want big living rooms, and so on. The architect's role is to bring balance to the process and accord each living area its proper due while keeping the entire project under budget, on schedule, and up to the aesthetic standards set by the architect and client together.

Public buildings go through the same process although in a somewhat less personal and individualistic way. Public space is a place where the sense of community is heightened and relationships are promoted between members of the public. Neutral corners are offered where specific tasks are carried out or thoughts are gathered for the work to be done. The balance between the two makes the role each space plays all the more effective.

As an architect, I like to look not only at the surface and shape of buildings, but at their underlying structures, too. Every building consists of beams, headers, and multiple other components that are concealed, yet play the more important role of supporting the structure. As a legislator, I can't help but see the same underlying structures in society except that they are intangible concepts, or values that connect individuals to their community—values like neighbor helping neighbor, that all of us are entitled to equal opportunity and freedoms, and that each of us must take responsibility for our actions and for keeping our nation strong.

ENHANCING THE REPUTATION OF THE DESIGN PROFESSIONS

"What is the ethical framework for design? Is 'good design' just an elitist rallying call, a sign of dissatisfaction with the judgments of the mass market? Or does 'good design' consist of a more humane, more free, and more delightful physical environment for everyone?"

BOONE POWELL, FAIA

Not too long ago, Mexican architect Ricardo Legorreta challenged an audience of architects to consider the recent track record of America's engineers and doctors. Legorreta noted that in this century, engineers have extensive road systems and bridges to their credit; as for the medical profession, the extraordinary advances of medicine have added years to our lives. Compare this, he went on, to the impact of this country's architects on the daily lives of most Americans.

Legorreta wasn't saying that today's architects lack the talent to design good, if not great architecture. From his perspective the issue is *who* or, more to the point, *how many* are served by this talent.

Quality design is not a luxury

As Legorreta sees it, it's typically the wealthy individual or large developer, not the community, who has access to the best today's architects have to offer. If his observation is correct—and I haven't met an architect who believes the profession has more work than it can handle—it doesn't take much imagination to predict the consequences of serving a shrinking client base.

From the public's standpoint, design that makes the spirit soar, while admired, is reserved for the privileged; it's a luxury or an expensive option, not a necessity. It touches the margins rather than the core of their lives.

Since the public has seldom been in the habit of commissioning the work of architects, does it really matter if the average citizen isn't standing in line for the profession's services? Perhaps it does. After all, how supportive is such a public going to be if, for example, its elected representatives are inclined (or not) to pursue the highest design standards for new public architecture? Or preserve a historic district? Or put in place a regulatory climate that encourages excellence?

But that's just the beginning of the harm done when the constituency for good design is small.

The wrong client calls the tune

When the design professions fall into the hands of a relative few who can afford their services, the motives of these few may be driven by profit alone or an "edifice complex" rather than service to the community. For every Jonas Salk who commissions Louis Kahn to design a project that celebrates the site it enhances, there are far too many clients whose view of their investment hardly rises above a limited vision of their own short-term return on investment.

The evidence for expediency or, on the other hand, conspicuous consumption is everywhere, from Main Street to the suburban shopping mall.

The lack of a community perspective goes some way to explain the tunnel vision of much postwar construction, a line of sight that does not strive to integrate a particular building or complex of buildings into a larger economic, transportation, social, and environmental context. There isn't enough ivy to cover the lamentable results. Slapped in the face by an especially bad project, the public's indifference to architects can deteriorate into outright hostility.

Serving the whole community

What is the most direct route that will lead architects from the margin into the heart of their community? There is no easy answer, but one thing is sure: we can no longer sit back and complain among ourselves that architects are not valued as an indispensable community resource. No one is going to make the case for design more persuasively than the design professions themselves.

Meeting that challenge belongs to those who have the will to renew themselves. And the first step down that road begins with a commitment to enhance the life of the community, a commitment most powerfully exercised by encouraging the client to take the largest, long-range view of a project. The value gained will be threefold, bringing rich dividends to the client, the community, and the public's appreciation of what is, after all, the most public of the arts.

"If our nation is to have sustainable competitive advantage in the global economy, then we must take [design] and its integration power seriously."

EARL POWELL

The designer's contribution to a project is all-too-often compared by the general public and clients alike to a cosmetician who applies the lipstick, rouge, and eyeliner to an otherwise plain face. What a shallow comparison! And harmful, too. Among the destructive consequences is the present climate in which the designer's services are undervalued as well as misused.

Making a persuasive case for the holistic, integrative process that is design looms as our biggest communication challenge. First, we have to reject a debased definition of design that equates it with style and fashion. Design is the blood and tissue, not just the lipstick and rouge. Design works from the inside out. It's as integral to the successful functioning of a whole project as skeletal and musculature systems are to getting out of bed in the morning and making that first pot of coffee. To ratchet up the image one more notch, the brand of coffee may be a luxury; a healthy body is not.

Design is more a means than an end

Not just aesthetics, but such issues as cost, equipment, color, function, technical capability, structural quality, material options, marketing, image, psychology, time factors, use, and much more—all are part of the design *process*. The process works like the images produced by a kaleidoscope: Change any one element, however small, and all the various other pieces spontaneously realign and produce a different outcome.

The designer's challenge and glory is to orchestrate every issue carefully and move the entire business to a successful result. Clients who value quality, reliability, and good business decisions require this kind of full service, full service that only a trained and experienced architect can provide. To compromise now is to reap later regrets.

> **Design is the source of energy that drives a dream across the finish line.**

On every side winning projects demonstrate that clients who are alert to their own best interests maximize their investment in design. They grasp the power of a design professional to spin straw into gold.

Design is not a fancy racing stripe. Whether the client is a homeowner or a Fortune 500 corporation, design is the source of energy that drives a dream across the finish line.

"A designer must be able to do a job as it should be done,
and he must understand it."

HANS J. WEGNER

Design is not an option-if you define "design" as the act of shaping our surroundings to accommodate our needs. Design is a strategy, an instinct, an essential tool for survival.

People are animals when it comes to shaping their surroundings-we often make a mess of it. We foul our own nests. The evidence is the ugliness that disfigures many of our cities and blights the countryside. What we see in the wreckage that confronts us on all sides is not the absence of design, but its nemesis-inappropriate or just plain bad design.

People can get it right

Paris, Tuscan villages, whole neighborhoods in Stockholm, Rockefeller Center, Fallingwater, the University of Virginia, Columbus, Indiana—all are dense with positive feelings. Each is a place that splendidly accommodates human needs. Each enriches and expands what it is to be alive.

One goes to such places to recognize our innate creativity and the love each of us is born with for the beautiful and the good.

People and places need designers

With only the market to guide it, design is often less a creative strategy than a blunt instrument. Instead of building on the best of yesterday while articulating a visionary agenda for tomorrow, bottom line expediency chips away at a community's assets. We settle for a quick profit, instead of demanding an investment in delight. We are driven by expediency. What then develops is the uglification of our communities.

In shaping meaningful experiences, in handling with skill the tool that is design, architects are servants of our better angels. Whether in traditional practice or in the expanding fields of industry, finance, and public service, they initiate and focus public dialogue about design options. They understand and practice the process of thinking well about problems. They foster the transformation of strangers into productive, vital, and livable communities. What now develops is the beautification of our communities.

Evangelists for good design

The challenge to architects is clear: They need to be evangelists for good design, all the while making clear that theirs is not an exclusive ministry, but a shared community responsibility.

How do we make the best case for good design? By example, of course. But that's only part of the answer. The case for good design must also be made from within existing institutions. I believe, for example, that when considering loan applications, the financial community should include architects on the review panel. Good or appropriate design is an accurate indicator of just how sound an investment really is.

The medium and the message

The same reasoning can be extended to the community as a whole. A public that understands the process that leads to design that makes the spirit soar will be able to discriminate among conflicting options. Once the relative merits of our choices are clear, self interest alone will lead us to shape our environments more wisely, guided by a community's most creative resource-its architects.

WITH A LOT OF HELP FROM OUR FRIENDS

"If you aren't encouraged where you work, find someplace to work where you will be. My friends didn't believe that I could become a successful speaker. So I did something about it. I went out and found some new friends."

JOE LAWSON

D on't believe all the claims of political candidates. In most human endeavors, the leader's role and real power are exaggerated. This is as true for those seeking public office as it is for architects.

Politician and professional alike, we're all carried along by larger forces. We don't determine the rise or fall of tides or which direction the wind blows. At best, by understanding these forces, we can make them work for us. With compass in hand, a knowledge of how to read navigational charts, and some skill at working the sails, we can cover vast distances and make the harbor of our choosing, instead of being broken on the rocks.

> *Strengthen ties with those who share your vision.*

One thing else: to go anywhere, we require allies and alliances. We need friends.

True leadership empowers others

During the tenure of J. Carter Brown and Jackson Walter, the National Gallery of Art and the National Trust for

Historic Preservation respectively enjoyed extraordinary growth. Brown went on to lead the Pritzker Prize jury and the Washington, D.C. Fine Arts Commission. Walter turned to historic preservation and transformed Waterford, Virginia, into a national model. That's good news for architects: Brown and Walter, each in his own way, greatly expanded the audience for design excellence. In doing so, they expanded the market for architects' services.

Who are the Browns and Walters in your community? What institutions or organizations do they represent? And, most important, are you cultivating meaningful relationships with them?

Whether we are architects, preservationists, or museum professionals, the challenge we face in making the world a more hospitable place is too large for any one of us alone. Architects owe it to the public they serve to strengthen their ties with those who share their visions. Only then can all of us hope to move closer to a shared goal-a world made better by design.

PULLING TOGETHER,
NOT APART

"A poster I've shared with groups for years is titled, 'Teamwork.' In Scene One, two mules are tied to one another by a rope. They're facing in opposite directions, sniffing different stacks of hay. In Scene Two, they begin to try to reach their goals but have no luck. The rope is too short and they're pulling against one another. In Scene Three, it seems the harder they pull, the harder it is to reach their goals.

"In Scene Four, they have turned around, sitting down now and looking at one another, probably thinking, 'Hey! If we can just get our acts together instead of pulling against one another, something good could happen.' Then in Scene Five, they eat one stack of hay together and in Scene Six, they accomplish the second goal as they eat the other haystack together.

"The sad thing is, there are so many groups living in Scene Three, pulling against each other and it seems the harder they work, the harder it is to reach their goals."

CARL MAYS

W hat forces are pulling against the influence of the design professions, and how effectively are America's designers pulling from the other side?

In my experience, professional associations are the most important resource a designer has to get a grip on the forces transforming how we communicate, negotiate, and meet the client's expectations. Pulling together may not be the only way the individual designer prospers in today's world, but it certainly gives us a good shot at having the strength and stamina to come out on top.

Next, architects and designers should affiliate with the organizations that their clients are active in. Doing so makes the designer a magnet—a caring expert inside the field drawing the client toward wise decisions.

Finally, if you intend to achieve success within the design professions, affiliate with or create a team of fellow professionals. Don't ever think you are out there all alone.

Indifference and apathy are forces working against good design in our communities. Designers pulling together see things that could be and should be, and work to make them reality. Be a fixer—not a finger-pointer.

MULTICULTURAL ENERGY

"Valuing diversity means truly welcoming the uniqueness of each human being. In this we will greatly empower our communities and our markets to move forward."

HARRY ROBINSON, FAIA

It's not enough to pay lip service to the ideal of equal opportunity. It's not enough to feel good about saying the right things about cultural diversity. And it's not enough if, after the talking is done, the design professions do not mirror the diverse people we serve.

It's been well over thirty-five years since the executive director of the Urban League, Whitney M. Young, Jr., stood before The American Institute of Architects' national convention and challenged architects to be a truly inclusive profession. Over three decades and several committees and task forces later, progress is being made. But the profession does not yet reflect society's cultural diversity.

A snapshot of today's profession would show some new faces. The number of minorities, however, remains far too small. Frankly, that poses a danger: All the design professions risk becoming irrelevant as a force for positive change. To put it another way, if we don't change course, we're likely to end up where we're going.

The time has come for action

Design firms can be America's conscience. Look to the actions of the late Walter Blackburn, Jack Travis, and

Kohn Pederson Fox Associates. Their goal is to reflect the rainbow that is the reality of today's America. Only then will designers be positioned to be positive agents of change within the construction industry and society as a whole.

Our own individual path is equally clear: An honest commitment to equal access to the profession and respect for diversity will be measured not by the sound of our prose, but by the poetry of the action goals we have set for ourselves.

Having said this, the question becomes what action goals are we in fact setting for ourselves? Without a commitment to action—action that can be measured in the way we practice architecture—the rainbow will be an elusive goal.

A chance to energize the profession

Simply opening doors is not enough to truly welcome what former Herman Miller chairman Max DePree imaginatively calls "God's mix." It's not enough to guarantee our viability, not when an overview of today's architecture students shows that "God's mix" is tomorrow's profession. It's a high-octane brew that can energize all of us.

What a privilege to embrace it!

TODAY, ADVOCATE SOMETHING TRULY IMPORTANT

> "Like Jonathan Livingston Seagull we must have the
> conviction of our actions to get the greatest results.
> As confidence builds, we soar to new heights."

C. JAMES LAWLER, FAIA

Architectural historian Spiro Kostof wrote that architecture can be seen as "the material theater of human activity," and "its truth is in its use." To be an architect is an awesome responsibility. However, it is a shared responsibility, since the "truth" of good architecture is the outcome of teamwork. The owner, the contractor and subcontractors, the engineer, and interior designers—all work together to construct what will be used by groups as small as families and as large as entire nations.

The oft-quoted phrase by Winston Churchill, "we shape our buildings and our buildings shape us," perhaps best describes how important the act of design is. Architecture grabs us in ways we are often not conscious of; yet behavior, mood, and human activities are enriched by the success of the form and the function of a structure. Human emotion resonates with the physical properties of a building to create an uplifting, energizing response that transcends the practical requirements of the occupants. <u>Good architecture</u>

fulfills deep emotional needs; it confirms the aspirations of the human spirit.

This is what delights the public about the churches of Christopher Wren and the houses of Frank Lloyd Wright.

If design is this important to the *quality* of human activity, then enlisting the services of design professionals must not be limited to large and well-funded projects. Our experience within and outside of the smallest and most simple of structures can be greatly enhanced by the transforming power of the architect's creativity.

This transforming power is not limited to human delight. Since design is an exercise in problem solving, it follows that good design is a smart business investment. Time and again clients report that the services of a skilled design professional saved them money in the initial costs and especially in the life cycle costs of the building.

> *Architecture fulfills deep emotional needs; it confirms the aspirations of the human spirit.*

But the value the architect brings to the ultimate client, the public, is calibrated on a far larger scale. Architecture is, after all, about making places for human activity and contributing to the enhancement of the activity. Or, as Jon Ruskin wrote, "All architecture proposes an effect on the human mind, not merely a service to the human frame."

More than ever those who understand and have experienced firsthand the power of good architecture should actively promote its art and science. In both Eastern and Western cultures there are forces working against quality and good design. In the presence of the long shadow cast

56 by the quick return on investment and business expediency, no member of the design team can afford to miss opportunities to speak out on behalf of good design.

Instead of suffering such darkness, each of us must light a candle of advocacy in whatever private or public forum we have access to. With each spark struck, we will be lighting the way for future generations. Our gift to them will be an environment that fosters their physical, mental, and spiritual health. Surely we could not leave our children a more liberating legacy.

A candle of advocacy.

HONORING EXCELLENCE: DOING THE RIGHT THINGS

EXCERPTS FROM A SPEECH GIVEN TO HONORS GRADUATES AT CLEMSON UNIVERSITY

James Barker's letter inviting me to speak to you described this as your Honors Day. What could I say, I asked myself, that would add anything to this red-letter moment in your lives? As I ran through a mental list of possible insights—the global marketplace, service to the community, megatrends shaping your future—I kept coming back to the word itself—"honors."

The dictionary defines "honors" as "a showing of merited respect,...a ceremonial rite or service,...an academic distinction conferred on superior students." As I thought about what I was reading, it occurred to me all three definitions share a common denominator: "conferring," "showing," and "rites" all imply an event in which the public or the community plays a key role.

Up until this moment, most of you have labored more or less on your own. You've done your work-the research, the papers, your various projects-in a library, study hall, or at home. You've drunk a lot of coffee and wolfed down cold pizza under conditions not unlike solitary confinement. That's behind you. Today the cameras are clicking; the action is applause—lots of it—and it's all deserved, very deserved, because you are special.

What a validation for all the hard work and long hours! Here you are, surrounded by family, faculty, and friends. A lot of you will have write-ups in your hometown newspaper. Today is going to be a permanent part of your public resume.

Like an Olympic athlete, you're standing on a high platform. You've gone for the gold.

And like that of the athlete, the view from the top is great!

But if it *is* special, that means it's also out of the ordinary. An event like this doesn't happen often; our honor's days are rare.

Most of life is very different. The reality is the weeks, months, and years of hard, lonely training before you earn that brief moment of center stage. It's hours, long hours of study and studio.

Life is also the aftermath—the sweeping up of the confetti, the good-byes you say after your friends shake your hand one last time and then leave to return to their own lives.

If only you could capture this feeling that you have now, today, this *public* affirmation of your success. If only you could distill it and put it in a bottle. Then you could pour out a spoonful to get you over life's disappointments, wrong turns, and projects that never see the light of day.

As many of you have already discovered, public recognition for your best shot isn't inevitable. In fact, you may reap pain in the very fields in which you had carefully planted hope.

This came to mind when I read a story in *The Wall Street Journal* last week that had as its headline: "Being a Landlord Is a Mixed Blessing for Chicago Church."

The reporter was writing about Reverend Donald Sharp and the congregation of Faith Tabernacle Baptist Church. Reverend Sharp had been looking for a way that his predominantly middle-class flock could do something for the inner city.

A rundown mid-sized apartment building on Chicago's South Side seemed to be the answer. The church would buy it, fix up the twenty-four units, and offer affordable housing for the poor. It was an idea a whole community could rally around.

So nearly a year ago to the day, on April 12, the church had itself a new property and their minister was a hero. "We'll work with you," said the head of the tenants' association. Another woman gave Reverend Sharp a hug.

> *It's risky to listen for applause to validate your actions. It can lead you to count the esteem of others instead of your own self-respect.*

No doubt he felt like you're feeling now. He did the right thing and he was being deservedly recognized for his good work. It must have been great!

But a lot can go wrong with even the best intentions and the hardest work. Listen to how the reporter describes the weeks that followed the initial hugs:

> The maintenance man the church hired to live at the building noticed heavy traffic in and out of two apartments and suspected drug dealing.
>
> What's more, the two families under suspicion hadn't been paying their rent

for more than six months. Mr. Sharp had them evicted.

But they didn't exactly leave; they moved in with two other families in the building. Then, their children threw stones through windows of the vacant apartments. They set trashcans afire. When the disruptions continued, the church had the two other families evicted.

"It was very painful," recalled Mr. Sharp. "It seemed like we were running against the grain of what we wanted to do."

You have to feel for the guy. There's no way that last year's hugs and applause are going to get one through that kind of situation. And there is no way that even the wonderful energy that's in this room today is going to get us through the inevitable low points of all of our experience.

The point I'm making is that you can't depend on recognition and applause from others. Even when it does come, it's fleeting and soon becomes as distant as last week's headlines. Instead, you've got to be your own cheering section.

Of course, you can look to positive role models for guidance. You can seek the advice of trusted friends. But in the end, the reality is pretty stark: you're hanging out there on your own. Out there on your own you've got to be able to reach down deep, really deep inside yourself to find the courage to do what's right.

Something else: After you've acted, you have to have the good sense to pat yourself on the back. And then move on.

Maybe it's just as well you can't bottle the feeling in this room. It's risky to listen for applause to validate your actions. It can be addictive. It can lead you to court the esteem of others instead of your own self-respect. To trim your sails to catch the latest puff of an opinion poll is to be little more than another weather vane.

It's a message a lot of our politicians haven't gotten. That's why there's so much discontent these days. Instead of statesmen, we have weather vanes that swing now this way, now that, depending on where they see the advantage. You can't afford that, either in your profession *or* your personal life.

If there is one resource you must have to be truly successful in life—and by that I emphatically do not mean wealth or fifteen minutes of being a celebrity—it would be this: A strong set of values, a deep inner sense of ethics that provides the moral compass to steer you forward in a true direction with confidence.

You'll want that compass. You'll want to hold a true course in your relation to family, to friends, and the professional associations you develop in your life. You need it when you're trying to choose between conflicting courses of action when there's no professor around to grade you and no Honors Day to confirm the wisdom of your choice.

Most of our lives are not lived before an admiring audience. They are lived in the privacy of our thoughts.

Your family has provided the resources to bring you to this university. So it is fitting that they are honored today along with you. Your teachers have provided you with the knowledge that will be the basis upon which you eventually

[handwritten margin notes: 1. strong sense of values 2. inner sense of ethics — moral compass]

62 earn your professional reputation. So it's fitting that they, too, are being honored.

But the hard work that remains is up to you. Only you can respond to the deepest challenge of life, which one poet described as the vale of soul making.

There will seldom be applause for the effort of soul making. The very act of soul making will at times bring us into conflict with conventional wisdom, which surely is conventional but seldom wise. However, if you've done your job well, you won't be dependent on public approval before you act. You won't be looking over your shoulder; you'll be looking into the mirror of your heart.

There's a wonderful story that the late Nathaniel Owings, an AIA Gold Medal recipient and one of the founding partners of the architecture firm Skidmore, Owings, & Merrill, told about an extraordinary engineer by the name of Fazlur Khan, himself a recipient of numerous awards.

The story takes place in the 1950s, during the era of urban renewal and the first blush of the national interstate highway system. The highway engineers at the Department of Transportation had a scheme to carve up Washington, D.C., with concentric rings of inner, middle, and outer beltways. Destinations were irrelevant in the face of a commitment to perpetual motion.

The inner beltway was to dive under the Lincoln Memorial and then come up for air amidst the cherry trees at the Tidal Basin. Even the government's transportation experts realized something special was called for in designing the proposed bridge for such a site. So this great engineering talent Fazlur Khan was asked to propose a solution.

Think of the recognition and the prestige, not to mention the *money*!

If Kahn gave much thought to these, they weren't uppermost in his mind when he finally responded. He looked at the site and said: "Don't build it!"

Kahn's greatest monument in our nation's capital is something he never designed. Not a single stone marks the spot where his courage, his integrity, and his civic mindedness kept this piece of beauty from being vandalized for future generations. He lost the money; but he kept something that could never, ever be taken away from him.

I haven't told you how the story in *The Wall Street Journal* ended. In one sense, the conclusion of Reverend Sharp's ordeal hasn't been written. But in another sense it has, because the story reveals the inner landscape of the man. It's a rich landscape that, if anything, is richer because it has weathered great disappointment.

Here's the final paragraph; it's Reverend Sharp talking:

> I had a dream the other night. This building was just a jewel. Sparkling.
>
> Some of the older folks were sitting in the backyard on new benches and I was shooting pool down in the basement with some of the kind....I could have died after that, knowing that I'd made a difference.

It doesn't take public recognition to know we've made a difference. It doesn't take someone else's applause, nor does it take the speeches, the ceremony, and the wonderful excitement of a day like today to demonstrate what would be our most demanding critic—*ourselves*—that we've done well.

Real success, the kind that will not slip away once the applause has died down, is the difference our dreams make to the quality of our own lives.

Remember this day. Treasure it. It truly is special. But don't depend on it. Don't depend on it as you embark on your personal journey to achieve excellence. The sound that will ring most true in your ears as you navigate the high and inevitable low points that are sure to follow this special day, the words that will count will be your own inner voice saying, "I did my best!"

EMBRACING CHANGE

FAY JONES, FAIA

✳‑✳✳Architecture is invention—is innovation—but it is also...remembering.

As modern architects building for the future, we can continually learn from the abundant offerings of the buildings past, from the organizing principles they reveal and, in so doing, once again connect our architecture to that great body of rich contributions to our cultural heritage made by historical architecture. Any bridges to the future must connect with the past.

If one sees architecture as a continuum-as a belief in the continuity of the past and present...and future...then part of the pleasure of this work will lie in the creative connections he can make between that work and its sources-sources not simply quoted but transformed. Various influences can be melded into modern idioms that acknowledge and pay respect to sources, but also provide ways of creating new and appropriate settings for contemporary life.

In our search for appropriate archetypes, there is no richer source, or more fulfilling study, than the history of architecture. It is the clearest index to any civilization. In the richness of the past we can find innumerable models from which to extract structural and spatial forms—and compositional arrangements—which, through imaginative and rational transformations, can serve to solve our modern problems of building—and can serve and appropriately express our own practical and spiritual needs.

In the future—in the acceleration of a changing world-whatever the sources of creativity—whatever stirs our imagination-however we shape the things we do—whatever architectural language we choose to speak—it must somehow express something more than stylistic notions and mere accommodations. Its expression must transcend mere building, mere construction, mere technical achievement. As architects, we have the potential to build beautiful, well-composed places, large and small, that will not only accommodate our functional needs, but will stand as models which represent the best of our ideas. We have the power—and the responsibility—to shape new forms in the landscape—physical and spatial forms that will illuminate and nourish and poetically express our human qualities...at their spiritual best. As architects, as transformers of our living environment, we must eventuate that potential.

creative connections btwn past & future.

NORTHERN LIGHTS

"Recognizing a good idea is easy. Implementing it is quite another matter…[I]ncreasingly, design is being seen as a key component of marketing and corporate strategy…[H]owever, there must also be effective management of design for its potential to be realized." \

THE STANFORD DESIGN FORUM

A few years ago, I was invited to speak at a conference in Sweden by the Swedish Council for Building Research and the Architectural Society of Sweden. This gave me an opportunity to listen to others speak on subjects ranging from Nordic design to industrial architecture. The experience was the equivalent of a good sweat in a sauna topped off by a bracing roll in the snow. The passion Scandinavians have for good design is so contagious that I frequently recommend to friends, especially architects, that they consider Scandinavia for their next professional development experience.

The first invigorating jolt is to discover that the Scandinavians make an instinctive connection between value and excellence. And for value received, they are prepared to pay not what they regard as a premium, but a fair return on a service delivered. The prevailing view is that good designers should be fairly compensated. In certain other places around the globe, owners and project leaders are far more likely to concentrate *solely* on the goal of completing a building on schedule and keeping within budget.

This is not to minimize the importance of economics. Whether the site is Sweden or Sydney, owners everywhere apply economic criteria in order to determine whether an investment should be made. A certain minimal return is expected. Architecture, it must be remembered, is not an end in itself except in certain infrequent circumstances. So, buildings must be justified by economic quantifiable effects such as profitability and practicality and value as defined by the owner and ultimately the users.

Capital investment is typically looked upon in relatively short-term perspective, usually five to fifteen years in the private sector. Understanding longer term less tangible benefits requires a more sophisticated client. But those who are successful building owners in Sweden have discovered real value and benefits in the design *quality* of a project. Well-designed buildings have high occupancy even during economic recessions. Well-designed buildings have a long life and the potential for alternative utilization. They can have flexibility designed in them, so that the value of the original investment is protected from obsolescence. In short, the Scandinavians see the designer as an economic multiplier, not an optional expense.

Scandinavian architects make the case that good design is profitable for both the buyer and seller. Understanding the client's economic needs, they speak in the language of economics, but raise the level of the dialogue by placing the design process at the center of the discourse. They know how to calculate design in terms of needs, expectations, cost, output, and future options.

Looked at in this light, the Scandinavians are simply reinventing with new vigor the architect's traditional role. It's a dream architects share around the world. The difference in Sweden is that here it's actually working time after time.

There's no reason it can't be the same worldwide.

HARNESSING THE ENERGY OF CHANGE FOR ENTERPRISE

"Good design management is as much a matter of asking the right questions as it is of answering them."

AROL WOLFORD, HON. AIA

S ome management consultants are telling architects that they're losing their competitive edge; other, more aggressive members of the building team are eating their lunch. In the near future, it's going to be difficult for architects, they say, because of fundamental changes in project delivery and changes in the client's perception of efficiency.

The message is clear: this is no time to sit back. What's "normal" is being redefined. In that fact lies a paradox: What threatens traditional practice is at the same time an opening for breakthrough thinking and future success.

Of all professionals, the architect should be in the best possible position to seize the inevitability of change and transform its energy into a strategy of enterprise. After all, architects are near the top of the prestige list of all occupations, according to University of Chicago and *Money* magazine studies. The public sees architects as innovators, problem solvers, and among the most fascinating professionals in the world. That makes them valuable to all the rest of us non-architects who are trying to negotiate the twists and turns of the emerging new world.

For instance, architects are essential to anyone who has money to invest but wants to sweeten the odds of their success in the face of increased risks. Another example? Architects are—or should be—indispensable resources to those who want to build and improve the environment. There are more examples, but the point remains the same: There's a large and growing pool of potential clients being stirred up by the currents of change.

The best advice is sound, visionary business practice

But how does the profession translate the "should bes" into winning business strategies? How does an architect swim into the deep end of the pool without getting in over his or her head?

> ❝ *The hallmark of a well-run office is both fairness and perceptive negotiating skills.* ❞

First, there must be a commitment to learning the best skills to run a successful practice. Foremost that means being on the leading edge of the art and science that is today's architecture. No one trait will argue better for an architect getting the job than a reputation for competency.

However, these days the term for "best skills" embraces not only what goes on in a designer's head, but also how the office is run. And the hallmark of a well-run office is both fairness and perceptive negotiating skills.

As artists, architects are naturally competitive, as I can attest from years of listening to architects critique the work of their peers. However, architects are also in the business of enterprise. Here, for whatever reason, competitiveness does not seem to come as naturally. Architects need to work on entrepreneurial and competitive skills.

Negotiate for success

Skillful negotiation must be an important part of every architect's expertise. Clients expect it. After all, negotiation is a language they speak.

To be skillful at negotiation calls for practice. Decide on your objectives and strategy before you sit down with the client; then communicate clearly and stick to your plan. Winging it may get you the job, but getting by through sheer luck will turn out to be more harmful to your longer term objectives. You'll be perpetuating bad and ultimately defeating habits.

Believe there are solutions

The message of a skilled negotiator—that you can deliver success and measurable value to your clients—is what clients need to hear before they make an investment in your services. Communicating a "can do" attitude sets the right tone for a positive relationship, a relationship which, if skillfully cultivated, will lead to other jobs with that client.

Smart negotiators also communicate a clear commitment to growth. Clients look for that. It drives the vision statement that helps define your practice.

Looked at in this light, the preparation that goes into becoming an effective negotiator has implications larger than client relations. Vision, a commitment to growth and planning, a real familiarity with writing and speaking skills, a "can do" approach to any problem—they're all part of the negotiator's art. But they're also the vital signs of a well-run practice and a profession poised to harness the energy of change to power future success.

"The need for change bulldozed a road down the center of my mind."

MAYA ANGELOU

These days all professions are being redefined. But not everyone is comfortable with change. Some equate change with fear and crisis.

Crisis is an overly sensational view. It's also beside the point. Change is inevitable. The important question for architects to ask is: Will the new definition of their profession be broader, will it bring more responsibility?

I think it *must*. The alternative—a narrower definition, a predisposition to being spooked by the threat of liability—is out of the question if the profession is to have a viable future.

Change can bring back strength

In the course of the last two decades, I have been fortunate to be able to visit hundreds of firms each year. Many of these firms were going through top to bottom transformations. Sadly, a few of these firms are now out of business. Others, however, are today truly exciting places. Change brought those winning firms new strength and vitality, which they are able to pass along to their clients.

This is an important point: in firms large or small, architects become successful by helping their clients negotiate the same forces of change transforming every aspect of their own lives. They bring to a challenge their training, experience, and a knack for innovative thinking.

Some designers talk a good game about innovation and then don't deliver. They don't walk the talk. They cling to what it was in their history that got them to this point in time. Ironically, their greatest enemy may be their past success. Riding the rails instead of learning how to fly can be fatal because architecture as it was practiced five years ago is no longer relevant to serving clients' needs today. Real estate practices have changed; red tape has increased; the economy and financing methods are significantly different. The marketplace has new parameters and technology is altogether different. What all this adds up to depends on how you calculate: for some, this is a liberating time; for others, it's downright ugly.

Viewing change as a friend

In today's world of tight budgets, many architects are finding creative ways to deliver increased value. These architects are building stronger relationships where it matters. Many are actually delivering more than they promised their clients. In the changing marketplace, architects who are making change their friend are exploring new ways of being profitable and expanding their business plans.

> **Coach your staff about the urgency of change.**

Does this sound like your practice? If not, don't despair. You can use the energy of change to transform your career. If the responsibility is yours, so is the opportunity.

Set up a plan today to bring your practice up to its full potential. Make it fresh and creative. Don't allow yourself or the people you work with to become stale. Lead a rush of new ideas. Coach your staff and talk about the urgency of change. Pay attention to the way you manage time and make time to have more contact with your clients and the business community. You'll become a trusted resource and a valued partner.

Pursue open communications with your clients before, during, and after a project is completed. Listen to the feedback. Be especially eager to learn from your mistakes.

Architects and their clients can win big when there's mutual trust. Competence, creativity, and a commitment to team building are what today's clients are looking for when they're deciding how to invest their dollars. They're the leading cards that can make you a winner in the game of change.

PREPARING FOR SUCCESS

"No school would claim that it is perfect, and all are aware that there are severe problems with the Practical Training Scheme. Are practice and industry similarly aware of their responsibilities and critical of their performances in training and intern programs?"

ROYAL INSTITUTE OF BRITISH ARCHITECTS, STRATEGIC REPORT

Ten years ago a graduate from Virginia Tech moved to northern Virginia where he soon became an associate member of The American Institute of Architects. His wife, Gina Bottoms, was a teacher in the Fairfax County schools. I had an opportunity to talk to this young couple about career paths and what architecture in the future might be like. It was one of the most energizing dialogues I've had in a long time because this couple has a vision of success. In addition to a good education, Matt Maio has hands-on construction experience. He also has a global perspective thanks to a travel fellowship to Japan. Of course, he keeps his tech skills current.

He talks enthusiastically about the prospects of a career in architecture—but only if those taking the plunge are preparing for success. As he sees it, the successful architecture firm of the future will have the flexibility to seize opportunities quickly. Such firms will also be more entrepreneurial, highly automated, and especially adapted to meet the needs of what he calls the "new client."

Matt Maio is right: architects and designers must be willing to understand the world that is changing around them—and to accept new ways of practice. In some instances, they must challenge conventional wisdom. They must have a passionate commitment to successful design, but also to new ways of creating and delivering these designs.

Most of Matt's career is still ahead of him. I have no doubt that he will be successful because he has the perspective of a winner. He knows how buildings are made. He knows the requirements of the business side of the picture. He is looking ahead with an attitude of optimism. Most important, he knows how to communicate with people. There's not one small speck of arrogance associated with him. He is a mentor to others in the spirit of the design plus enterprise model.

The value of knowing how to inspire, motivate, manage, and serve people will be everything to the architect of the future; the value of know-it-all arrogance will be nonexistent. There's no more important lesson for schools of architecture to teach.

TAKING OWNERSHIP OF
YOUR OWN DESTINY

"If you see in any given situation only what everybody else can see, you can be said to be so much a representative of your culture that you are a victim of it."

S.I. HAYAKAWA

"In the age of information, survival still depends on hunters and gatherers." The words come from *The Wall Street Journal*. If this really is the information age, how well do most of us hunt and gather? According to Peter Schwartz, author of *The Art of the Long View*, not very well.

Part of the problem is habit; it's also laziness. We tend to look at life through the spectacles of what we already know. "What if?" isn't always an instinctive way of thinking about the future. Accepted wisdom isn't questioned nearly enough. We filter experience through prior conceptions. Our networks are less of a communications resource and more of a cocoon.

Ask what if A LOT MORE!!

The pitfalls of the pendulum

For example, in the face of a setback, how many of us have heard colleagues counsel patience, rather than new, breakthrough thinking? After all, they say, isn't the construction industry cyclical? Sooner or later, they promise, things will get better; the problem, whatever it is, will go away. The pendulum will inevitably swing back and we can pick up where we left off.

Unfortunately, neither life nor architecture is much like a clock. If there is any one thing we can set our watches by, it's this: The future will be better, worse, or different. What it won't be is the same. Risk breakthrough thinking within the new paradigm of design plus enterprise.

To hold our collective breath and wait for the sun to shine misses the fact that our planet is always moving. When the clouds break, we had better be ready to respond wisely and appropriately to a changed landscape, for changed it will surely be.

How can we make ourselves ready?

A key first step is figuring out what prevents us from thinking creatively about the future. One of the most powerful constraints is an unwillingness to probe the unimaginable, to try our hand at "what if" thinking—environmental needs, technology changes, the consequence of retired baby-boomers on social security, genetic engineering, global economic shifts, new service delivery models, and the like.

> *In a world where the only constant is change, we are either hostages or pathfinders.*

But if our radar is working at full capacity, we're ready to pick up unexpected technological, social, economic, and environmental blips likely to transform our practice—not to mention our world. A keen, open-eyed sense of what's shaping our tomorrow liberates us from self-made cages. It prepares us for opportunities. It opens us to change.

"Change" is the operative work here. In a world where the only constant is change, we are either hostages or pathfinders.

In my periodic meetings with the Business Roundtable and the U.S. Chamber of Commerce, I have come to realize that the client community is actively seeking pathfinders who understand twenty-first century issues and can shape change itself. The heritage of the design professions is that of shapers. If we expand our vision to understand, embrace, and shape change itself, we will be free to find our way and be a signpost for those we serve.

THE SUCCESSFUL FIRM

M. ARTHUR GENSLER, FAIA

People often ask me how you control a large firm. You don't. I learned a long time ago that to build a great organization, you hire people smarter than you are and then get out of the way. I'm honored to have such a collaborative, entrepreneurial, talented, creative, and energetic team.

People also ask me if I anticipated the amazing growth of our firm. The answer is, of course, "No," but I always find myself adding that growth is not the issue. Providing our clients with responsive design solutions is the issue, and the real trick is to do this across a closely linked network of offices. Everything we are today is attributable to our clients—not just because they give us the opportunities, but because they encourage us to learn from them, grow with them, go with them across the country, and then across the globe. Because of this, we've always been quite fearless in pushing the envelope of architectural services. We were fortunate to start our firm with a focus on work that fell below the radar for many architects—space planning and interiors. Hopefully, we had some effect on these services being a significant part of most firms' work today.

We currently have over 2,000 active clients, many for over twenty years, and, luckily for us, they are a roster of the world's leading companies. Most of these organizations are changing dramatically. As their world changes, ours is changing, too, constantly expanding the horizons of our work and our services. Our clients look to us now to develop business solutions,

(handwritten margin note: client based perspective)

based on an understanding of their business. They look to us to design projects that align with their business strategies. They understand, more than they did ninety years ago, that the quality and performance of their facilities are as critical to their success as their people, process and their technology.

Architecture knits these strategic elements together. And this is why today our profession has a unique opportunity to recapture our leadership role. Whether we're talking about a large or a small firm, this is the profession's time—and we must seize it. If we fail to do so, others will come forward. If we take the lead, they will follow. Together we can make a better world, a world in which we will all prosper.

architecture knits strategic elements together.

THE GOAL-ORIENTED FIRM

"Whether you think you can or think you can't,
you're probably right."

MICHAEL BOLINGER, FAIA

Each month I make a point to visit a number of architectural, interior design, and landscape architecture firms. I tour the facility, meet the people and typically have lunch with the principals and sometimes the entire firm. No two firms are ever alike.

Some, however, are unforgettable places because of their high goal-oriented culture. This becomes apparent in the first fifteen minutes of the visit. There's a strong hand on the rudder, guiding the entire enterprise in a sure, dedicated direction.

I often wonder why a commitment to clear, attainable goals is not universal. Maybe it is because it's just too obvious a strategy. The need for a vision or destination doesn't require genius IQ. It requires discipline and confidence. Clear instructions to staff should include a regular reminder of your fundamental vision of success. You will know your priorities when a clear picture of your goals is attached. Goal setting works.

Before reading this chapter, revisit your goals and action plan. A good designer *always* has an action plan.

In our research we discovered that there is not a firm in the country experiencing success who is not in the habit of

regular goal setting. Each week the firm reviews progress
and makes adjustments. Over time the goals change and
often expand. A new spirit of satisfaction permeates the
firm's culture.

A NEW PARADIGM IN
ENTERPRISE

"Problems are what generate new form, workable form."

FORREST WILSON

R ecently I visited a medium-sized architecture firm in the southeastern United States. It has a reputation for sensitive and accurate historic preservation work and for delivering real value in commercial, institutional, and health care. It's a pleasant, cheerful firm that brings life to its site—a downtown storefront.

From what I've seen in my travels around the country, this firm is doing several things about as well as I've encountered anywhere else.

- They are positioned as a visible and available community resource that participates in the life of the city.
- They listen to their clients with a passion. The architects' response to the clients' needs results in creative solutions the whole community takes pride in. When community leaders participate in the design process, they take ownership and satisfaction. Word spreads that something of real value takes place with these architects.
- They recruit the best people around. I don't mean simply skimming off the top graduates from the most prestigious schools. The principals take an active role in searching the whole field. What they're after is the best fit for each person, and that, among other considera-

tions, means seeking out individuals who have a strong value system.

- They part company quickly with employees who don't do their job. Acting aggressively on this front is a management responsibility too often overlooked. Remember: other members of the firm do not want their work and the reputation of the business pulled down by non-performers. It's usually no secret who the dead wood is. The enterprising principals can't afford to neglect their responsibilities to those who look to their leadership.

- They energize to combat trouble constantly. As one of the principals said to me: "Architecture is one damn thing after another." Compare this to those who try to avoid trouble entirely; they're so busy watching their step that they get very little done. Expect problems every day and have fun with the challenge.

- They hold themselves accountable for successful outcomes.

accountable implies ability to act though!

The culture of a firm incubates either top performance or mediocrity. Enterprising firms find a style and energy that nurtures the most positive performance, performance that often exceeds the client's expectations.

Firms like this will often not only be profitable, they will reap the dividends of knowing they have been catalysts for community place-making.

> **Enterprising firms find a style and energy that nurtures the most positive performance.**

THE LEADERSHIP OF COLLABORATION

"Leaders who win the respect of others are the ones who deliver more than they promise, not the ones who promise more than they can deliver."

MARK A. CLEMENT

For generations of readers of Ayn Rand's *The Fountainhead*, Howard Roark's laugh became the signature of the modern architect: a self-confident, uncompromising loner—and not a little arrogant in the bargain.

I realize that at times one does have to stand alone. There are times when the only right thing is to turn defiantly against what passes for common sense and strike off on a different, independent course. That's one dimension of design leadership.

But it's not the whole picture. More often, leadership means taking people with you. From what I can see, that often means getting *behind* people, not on top of them.

In other words, effective leadership is an artful balance between ego and teamwork. It's a marriage between assertion and collaboration. For examples, one need look no further than a symphony orchestra. What might otherwise be a babble of woodwinds, percussion, string, and brass is skillfully woven into a seamless tapestry beneath the wave of the conductor's baton. But as any player would be quick

leadership an a balance of ego's teamwork

to tell you, without the assorted gifts of the individual musicians, the conductor would be aimlessly beating time in an empty concert hall.

The chemistry of catalysts

Leadership that both sets the tempo and coaches the individual players to perform as one is a complex art. It has a lot to do with individual style-what's often called "chemistry." But it's a special kind of chemistry, the chemistry of catalysts. Some of the rules for creating that chemistry are easy to spot. Here are half a dozen to remember that will make the design enterprise successful.

> *Leadership means getting behind people —not on top of them*

1. Look at a problem or challenge from the group's point of view.
2. Proceed on the belief that everyone has the potential to be a valuable partner.
3. Identify common ground.
4. Focus on where you want to be, rather than arguing about where you are at the moment.
5. Bring together a wide range of talent and experience.
6. Be flexible.

This is leadership that makes good music. It empowers and transforms. For those fortunate enough to be under its powerful influence, it makes them owners of a wonderful enterprise in which the team rather than the gifted soloist is the star.

Experienced designers understand the value of the team. Sometimes they watch and listen; sometimes they captain. The result is always the same: those who form a team to carry out the best ideas will successful.

"Expect more and you will get more."

HAROLD L. ADAMS, FAIA, RIBA, JIA

Perhaps you've heard some architects say you can't make a decent living in architecture, Nevertheless, there are thousands of architects from firm principals to designers of single-family residences, earning better than a decent living. It's time to get the word out about their success.

If an architect settles for the cliché that "architects don't make much money," the world will not disappoint that architect's low expectations. But if you believe that architecture is a profession based on value, you are positioning yourself to earn a living that honestly reflects the real value you deliver.

When the price isn't right

Recently I was on the telephone with a friend who happens to be a law firm principal. He was in shock. In his hand was the first billing from his architect; the shock was the fee—it was unbelievably low!

Did he take great pleasure in his unexpected windfall? Not at all. His opinion of his architect took a nosedive because the architect clearly had a low estimate of his own work.

> *Your actions should be guided by your expectations - not by your fears.*

Clients pay for value

The lesson is as obvious as it is frequently ignored: the kind of fee you negotiate says a lot about how you value your own work. Right up there with their creative and interpersonal skills, architects need to know how to establish value-based fees and how to negotiate effectively. The first time an architect negotiates confidently, sure of what he or she contributes to clients, that architect will make a happy discovery: clients are seeking value today; they want the professionals they choose to believe in their own worth.

Without profitability, the design professions have no future. What is the flip side of the substantial risks that hang over professional practice today? The substantial profits taking those same risks can generate.

The point is, don't buy the line that a career in architecture is a one-way ticket to the poorhouse. It just isn't so. Believe in the profession and yourself. Then your actions will be guided by your expectations, not your fears.

"Progress always involves risks. You can't steal second base
while keeping your foot on first."

FRED WILCOX

S ome designers are comfortable with significant
financial risk-taking; many are not. Risk, however,
is a prerequisite to breakthroughs in business as
well as art. Carelessness is not.

So before leaping headlong into the arms of risk, there
are some things to keep in mind:

- Unless there's a solid business plan promising that risks
  will be rewarded, I always urge caution before taking on
  debt. Be enthusiastic—but know how and when to say
  "no." A friend of mine recently quoted Dickens: "Make
  $10 a week, spend $9 and the result is bliss. Make $10
  a week, spend $11, and the result is despair."

- Budgets help make a firm run more smoothly, prof-
  itably, and confidently—if they're developed honestly
  and adhered to rigorously.

- Designers who are successful do not dig themselves into
  a hole of debt.

- Designers who are successful and want to diversify
  should seek out expert advice from those who have
  experience and success with new areas of diversifica-
  tion. Make the network work for you.

- Designers should cultivate a self-image of financial confidence. It's part of success and leadership.

- Design is an enterprise. Be informed. During a break from a design jury in the southern United States, I asked the other panelists about a recent *Wall Street Journal* article. No one had read it because they weren't in the habit of following the financial press. Give this notion a try: Forty percent of your reading should be outside of the design professions. Reading *Business Week, The Wall Street Journal, The Economist, Financial Times, Barron's,* and the like will sharpen your business skills and strengthen your firm.

> *Keep the long view and coach those around you to do the same.*

- Factor inevitable dry periods into your business plan. Let others be grasshoppers; your role should be that of the ant. Effective financial leadership calls for socking away some reserves for the inevitable rainy days. See the valleys as opportunities for breakthrough volleys.

All the above can be summarized by two words: be prepared. Keep the long view and coach those around you to do the same. With every economic and technological shift, there's always a shakeout period. Downturns don't have to be a death knell; they can be your wake up call.

Around the corner of every business cycle is an economic surprise. Anticipation and resiliency will be the key to your success. Responsibility and performance will be rewarded.

"I dwell in possibility."

EMILY DICKINSON

Some designers boast about earmarking up to 6 percent of their budget to market their firms. Not a bad idea, but try this concept: We should be talking about 100 percent!

Far from being an exact science, marketing is an all-encompassing art that demands a twenty-four hour commitment. Delivering the right message to the right audience with appropriate emphasis and tone is a seven-day-a-week challenge for everyone in your enterprise. Yes, including, and perhaps most importantly, even those who answer phones and greet visitors. First impressions count.

Interns should be shown the ropes of effective public relations the first day they begin work for an office. At the other end of the scale, principals must be high profile both inside and outside the office. From intern to firm principal, all staff should appreciate how much difference enthusiasm makes to clients.

Not one hour should pass without a conscious effort to market and promote the value of what you do and who you are. Get out the word there's a new definition of marketing operating in your firm and include responsibilities for marketing on everyone's job description. That's 100 percent of your staff!

Are marketing professionals needed in design firms? By all means. But don't for one minute think marketing is someone else's responsibility of a single line item. It's all, or nothing at all.

> "My vision of the future no longer relies on a world without troubles and cares. Rather it is a world where the challenges are realizable. Such a vision is based on a scenario in which the human imagination, drive, and competence combine to meet the enormous hurdles of, for example, environmental restoration."

PETER SCHWARTZ

W orry is a misuse of the imagination. There's a lot that's beyond our power to predict, perhaps almost anything that really matters. The future of the global economy; when or where the next natural disaster will strike; what will happen if I walk across town to a meeting instead of grabbing a cab?

I have conducted futures intervention workshops where we examine possible future scenarios and then begin to put our ideas together on just how we fit into each of them. The point is that even after putting together a good business strategy based on the best evidence available, it's smart to look at other scenarios and then think creatively about the reinventing and repositioning that would be necessary for success if the future handed us a surprise.

Thinking the unthinkable

Design firms must think the unthinkable at regular intervals. The decisions made at such brainstorming sessions

104   make a difference. They stretch the imagination. They prepare one to move with great agility and effect. They build a culture of anticipation.

Yes, there are people who have convinced themselves their choices do not matter. So they sit tight. *Que sera sera*, what will be will be. They're wrong. The simplest choice, whether to have lunch with a client or to further procrastinate on building relationships, can have a profound effect on determining our future. Getting the information together to make the most informed choices is important. It's a prerequisite of success.

Building future scenarios

There are numerous books that can help us acquire a proficiency in the art of developing what-if scenarios. One that I recommend is *The Art of the Long View* by Peter Schwartz. It is a handy guide to help the architect use the scenario building process to plan for the future in an uncertain world.

> *Prepare for the future and build a culture of anticipation.*

Thinking this way about the future pays off. The dividends are physical and creative resiliency. We're like an athlete in top form, ready to grab the ball no matter how it bounces. By becoming actively involved in planning our future, we ourselves become agents rather than objects of change.

Worry doesn't work. Creative anticipation does. It's a winning scenario.

BUILDING A COMMUNITY OF CREATIVITY

"You think you understand the situation, but what you don't understand is that the situation just changed —change is changing."

DOUG PARKER, AIA, HON. IIDA, HON. FASID

I recently returned from a visit with an award-winning firm in the Northeast who has lost some of their top younger talent. To their credit they have decided to make a commitment to regain their innovative ways—and to attract new talent into the firm. I'll stress right off that they have a strong platform to build on and they arguably have as good an external reputation as a firm can have. Moreover, they have a solid financial base with a management infrastructure that can leverage the power of a good idea. They are very well connected to the client community.

Nevertheless, there is a predicament. Upon close examination, this firm lost some of their youthful, energetic talent due to internal cultural elements. The studio atmosphere in this firm has lacked the inspiration formerly present and has failed to nurture their creative staff. The driving sense of mission and belief in the absolute meaningfulness of their work is lacking. This did not happen overnight. Gradually, almost imperceptibly, the firm lost the spirit that drives innovation.

How does it happen that one firm seems to catch fire while another goes flat? To that question, I'll share with you just a few of the key findings from discussions we had in this specific firm.

1. The firm possessed strong ethical values, but there was little internal communication between generations. Therefore, there was a lack of shared ethical values.

2. The design of the workspace fostered isolation, not innovation. People were not circulating in the interior spaces in ways that would foster shared ideas and brainstorming. Partners were in a separate area—the power wing—insulated from the studios.

3. There were numerous sacred cows built into the financial culture. Open book financial management was never implemented. Although the partners had talked about it, they reached the erroneous conclusion that many employees would "just not understand" certain elements of the business. The sacred cows became failure costs built into the budget. The firm unintentionally budgeted to fail—that is, to lose top younger talent.

4. The firm possessed a power-based hierarchy rather than knowledge-based empowerment of all employees.

The firm has decided to address these areas to become a stronger place to work and to nurture young, hot talent.

1. They have made a commitment to cultivate values inside the firm that fit their vision. The vision will not change—nor should it in this case—but the firm will

recognize creative achievements within a new organizational structure that stresses communication and value propositions internally as well as externally. Open book management will provide a feedback loop that measures what the firm values.

2. They have decided to continually question how they communicate, mentor, and lead. They have set up a new Intranet with an active chat room. And they are moving to a new office design—open and centered around the true meaningful work of the firm—rather than around transparent power structures.

3. They are evaluating their ownership structure—and looking for a transition. There are forces and behaviors that they want to encourage to sustain their creative, innovative cultural ambitions. They understand that there is no silver bullet to build their desirable innovative culture; still, they are committed to that innovative culture and to gradually doing what is necessary to foster enduring creativity.

Increasing a firm's creativity can be achieved through a community that establishes a vision and a value system that supports innovation in both individuals and teams. The key is establishing a connection with the changing client base and then putting in place the spatial and human ingredients for success. While no two firms are alike, inner dynamics can provide guidelines for all firms to dramatically increase creative performance.

SNATCHING SUCCESS FROM THE JAWS OF ADVERSITY

"Leaders are needed more in difficult times. In calm waters every ship has a good captain."

SWEDISH PROVERB

I had been asked to write a column for a professional newsletter during what was shaping up to be a difficult year for architects. I spent some time struggling with the shape of the message. I couldn't ignore the fact that many architects and their families had been mugged by a punishing recession that gave no indication of letting up. On the other hand, I didn't want to come off like Chicken Little, squawking about the falling sky.

That's when I re-read an intriguing card that had caught my eye the week before. It came from a New Jersey firm. The card was part of a mass mailing targeted to the firm's current and prospective clients. And that's where I found my message. Here are some examples of how one architect squeezed lemons into lemonade:

- "We have heard there is a recession; our firm is not participating. While other firms are downsizing, we are growing by finding new ways to help our clients take advantage of the recession."
- "Most contractors are bidding very competitively; recent projects have bid 15 to 25 percent lower than normal. Contractors are reassessing profit and minimiz-

ing overhead. If you are planning any kind of construction, maintenance, or repair projects we can help you to
take advantage of this outstanding bidding climate."

- "...If you are contemplating any kind of new project,
we can help you to be ahead of the competition by
preparing feasibility studies and obtaining the required
approvals."

- "...We can help you to grow by programming your
space requirements and organizational relationships in
order to use existing space more efficiently.....We can
economically enhance your organization's image, with
positive effect on clients and staff efficiency. We can
help you to consolidate several facilities into a single
location."

- "A time of slow growth offers an excellent opportunity...to perform a complete assessment of your facilities
and your plans for them...We can advise you on barri-
er-free construction and energy code compliance. We
can, in fact, prepare a comprehensive master plan for
your facilities. "Our aim is to serve all our clients' needs
on budget and on schedule. No project is too small or
too large for us."

Loud and clear

I haven't shared every sentence, but the upbeat message of
a can-do firm comes through loud and clear even in this
edited version. Congratulations to the thousands of design
professionals who find light when it's darkest and the will
to succeed in the midst of doubt.

THE POWER OF OVERESTIMATING YOUR COMPETITION

"Behavior that doesn't lead people forward and get them on the right track is needless behavior."

STEVE FISKUM, FAIA

I was at a firm out west not long ago, listening to the director of marketing outline her firm's plans for the coming year. She provided an oral short list of their primary competitors with some valid reasons why her firm was more qualified in just about every way. She said to me, "you know Jim, we are the best and we'll do almost anything to beat down those other firms." She had the right "fire in the belly" but her message was troubling because I've always felt that how you deal with your competition says a lot about you.

My timing wasn't exactly right but I decided anyway to make a case for professional civility right on the spot. "I would like to take issue with something you said," I started. "Arrogance has brought down many of the mighty barbarians—but firms who deflect, outsmart, and never underestimate their competitors are the ones I would bet my money on staying the strongest over the long term." She looked unconvinced as I continued, "these are firms with confidence and a commitment to professionalism... they have a capacity to both enjoy their work and to appreciate the work of their competitors."

Why did I say this? Because I believe that competition is instructive—and it makes for faster evolving design professions. We are fortunate to have so many strong design professionals in our society. Use the model of "competitive fitness," not "competitive advantage."

I believe that when you talk about the competition, you can acknowledge them like this: "I have heard that they too do good work." Then you can continue to expand on the key reasons that your firm is different. These expressed differences provide the conceptualization of what makes your firm special. You can take your concepts to the next level to discuss your vision and how you have a stubborn consistency in serving your clients in exceptional ways.

To be a competitor does not mean that you must be a bully. Quite the opposite. To succeed, it takes more than ego. Therefore, I'm suggesting that you make a habit of overestimating the competition because it is bound to help you in a variety of ways. When you overestimate the competition you will continually sharpen your own strate-

> *Overestimating your competition sharpens your own strategies.*

gies, standards, systems, and communications. Then, when you discover that your competitiveness is indeed strong, you will be prepared to always have an advantage, because you are anticipating going up against the best. From time to time you will be way out front and when that happens it is a pleasant experience.

Remember that the arrogance factor can be self-defeating. The confident and civilized rainmakers—not the "competitor crushers"—are ones getting today's—and tomorrow's—best projects.

UNDERSTANDING REJECTION'S STRATEGIC POTENTIAL

"Far better it is to dare mighty things, to win glorious triumphs, even though checkered by failure, than to take rank with those poor spirits who neither enjoy much nor suffer much, because they live in the gray twilight that knows not victory nor defeat."

THEODORE ROOSEVELT

Will you have a stronger year ahead or will you backslide? Many firms are asking themselves this question as they assess their capabilities within the changing marketplace. The future offers new challenges for every firm. Every week, several hundred firms learn they were not selected for a project they were going after.

For instance, for its new $130 million Central Library, the Minneapolis Library Board recently shortlisted seven teams. But the firms who did not make the short list also make for an interesting story. Rejected firms include Michael Graves, Arquitectonica, The Hillier Group, Hardy Holzman Pfeiffer, Ten+W (Enrique Norten of Mexico City), Julie Snow, Alsop of London with Cunningham Group, and Leonard Parker/Durrant with James Polshek and Partners. The rejected firms are now looking at other opportunities while the seven finalists will spend considerable time and money during next level interviews. All the firms who submitted qualifications believed they had a shot at the commission, yet all but one will be rejected. [The eventual winner was Cesar Pelli].

Consider the phenomena of rejection. Some firms miss out on strategic ideas because they don't understand that markets and clients' expectations are changing. Often, firms take a look at past experiences and then plan for next generation improvements. This assumes that change is incremental and linear. Change today is often non-linear and requires more than plans built around a firm's past experiences.

The turbulence, threats, and complexity of A/E/ID selection will likely increase in the future. Yet the opportunities in the future are gigantic. Firms need to ask themselves several key questions:

1. In what markets should we compete?
2. How should we compete in these markets?
3. Where do we allocate our resources, budgets, and investments to achieve success?

Identifying and sharing reasons for rejection is as important as sharing strategic potential. It is valuable because it builds a shared awareness of the firm's situation. This leads to thinking about options and strategies the firm should pursue. A top-performing firm will not likely abandon its market positions. An under-performing firm will need to change. All firms, though, want to step back from defeat, to put rejection into perspective, and to strengthen the firm's capabilities to insure that its markets and building segments are currently attractive.

Everybody gets rejected—several Pritzker Prize winners have been rejected more often than you have. Babe Ruth struck out at a record pace—but knew how to get results in other ways. Your challenge is to find the other ways that deserve exploration, decision, and inclusion in your success plan.

JUST SAY NO

"They're only puttin' in a nickel, but they want a dollar song"

SONG TITLE

It's never easy. For a young design firm, it might even seem inconceivable. But sooner or later there comes a time when you have to walk away from a potential client. The reasons for a parting of the ways are various: it may be because of fee, or chemistry, or conflict of interest. Whatever shape the challenge takes, always opt for the high road.

No designer is whole without a client. A prerequisite, however, is compatibility. If you don't sense compatibility, chances are you may not be able to add real value. In business as in marriage, there's little sense in pursuing a relationship that can't be satisfying for all parties. Look for shared expectations and a good fit when it comes to your values.

Even if the chemistry is there and the project is challenging in the best sense, if the fee is too low or if a client insists on a low hourly rate, simply and in the most friendly manner possible, walk. Always keep your goals in mind when it comes to profitability and value, and remember what it takes to give you success and piece of mind.

WHAT CLIENTS ARE LOOKING FOR

"The big salaries in business go to those who have what it takes to get things done. That is true not only of those who guide the destinies of business, but it is true of those upon whom they must depend for results."

J.C. ASPLAY

There is a world of new business opportunities for designers. However, as we have been discussing, the marketplace is changing constantly. About the same time as the architect is comfortable with offering a new line of services, there is yet another restructuring. It's frustrating, but it's life in today's design professions.

The good news is that for the foreseeable future, well into the twenty-first century, the market will expand. Yet this very expansion generates its own upheavals. One thing is sure: The traditional vision of the profession most architects were introduced to in school is a thing of the past.

A new vision—even more relevant service and value

While there is much anecdotal information about clients' attitudes, there has been little statistically reliable research in this area until recently. To remedy this situation, The American Institute of Architects has researched commercial and institutional clients' perceptions of architects and the perceived value of their services. The purpose of this research is to better understand what clients need, expect, and value in an architect, thereby providing architects with valuable insights into how to market and deliver services more effectively.

The research was conducted in two phases. Phase I began with a series of three focus groups with 33 participants representing commercial developers, businesses, schools, churches, health-care facilities, nonprofit entities, and government agencies. Held in Seattle, Chicago, and Atlanta, the focus groups examined how clients solicit and select architecture firms for projects and the presentation materials and techniques to which these clients best respond. The focus groups provided important information for phase II, a nationwide telephone survey of more than 800 medium-size health-care, education, and nonprofit institutions and businesses with 50 to 2,500 employees.

KEY FINDINGS

Architects have an overall positive image

It should come as no surprise to most people that architects are held in high esteem. More than 91 percent of the Roper survey respondents said that they have either a high or fairly good opinion of architects. Among 14 professions respondents were asked about, architects ranked in the top third, higher than building contractors and real estate developers, who rated in the middle third. Other studies such as those done by the University of Chicago have consistently agreed.

Architects are considered creative, but elitist and insensitive to budget issues.

While architects get high marks for being professional, creative, knowledgeable, experienced, and concerned about quality, clients indicated that there are several areas for improvement. When asked which of a series of 20 adjectives apply to architects, 7 in 10 respondents said the terms "demanding" and "elitist" describe architects completely or somewhat, and 6 in 10 said the term "arrogant" also applies.

In addition, the client respondents also believed architects need improvement in the area of money issues. While more than half said the phrases "budget sensitive" and "save you money" apply to architects completely or somewhat, a large number (43 percent) said that "save you money" does not describe architects too much or at all, and nearly one-third said the same about the phrase "budget sensitive."

Responsiveness to client and securing government approvals are key factors in architect selection, not fees

When selecting architects for projects, clients said they are looking for professionals who listen and respond well to their needs and goals and who are able to manage the complex maze of regulations, political approvals, and zoning requirements. More than 80 percent of survey respondents indicated that "responsiveness to the client" and "ability to manage zoning requirements" are the two most critical selection criteria of the 15 tested.

The architect's abilities to adhere to both schedules and budgets were next in importance (77 percent for each), followed by related prior experience, design quality, and concern for environmental issues. Architectural fees were ranked relatively low on the scale of selection factors. Clients seemed to feel that fees can be negotiated; chemistry, responsiveness, and an ability to listen cannot.

Health-care organizations place more emphasis on an architect's overall experience than the other groups surveyed. Seventy-five percent of the health-care professionals surveyed rated overall experience as "very important" compared to 63 percent of respondents overall.

The study indicated that responsiveness, experience, and ability are key factors in architect selection as well. In particular, they noted that how well the architect listens and responds to questions during presentations is crucial.

Clients are less appreciative of architects for pre- and post-design services

Architects are perceived as being valuable by both business and institutional clients for a wide range of services. Of the 12 categories tested, the most valuable areas to clients were designing a new building, space planning, and helping obtain zoning and building permits. Other architectural services valuable to clients were giving advice about energy efficiency and suggesting ways to save on construction costs. Areas where clients thought architects to be less valuable were pre-design services, such as

> **"*Whatever shape the challenge takes, always opt for the high road.*"**

programming and site selection, as well as managing construction projects, facility management, and help in obtaining financing.

One reason that many business and institutional clients may not turn to architects for pre-design, construction, and facility management services is that they may turn to their own staffs to provide these services. Although fewer than 2 in 10 of the clients surveyed said they have in-house architectural or design staff, more than 4 in 10 said they do have an in-house planning and/or project management group.

While the majority of clients surveyed who had undertaken renovation or new construction projects in the past 10 years did involve an architect, 17 percent did not. The most often cited reasons for not doing so were "the job was not big enough" and the work was "handled by in-house staff."

There are key differences between institutional and business clients

Institutional clients see a greater value in turning to architects for many services than do medium-sized businesses. Outside of traditional building design and permit functions, larger businesses—those with 1,000 to 2,500 employees—are less likely than medium-sized business and health-care, education, and nonprofit organizations to say that architects are very valuable for programming.

One reason for this may be that larger businesses are more likely to have either an in-house architectural or design staff or an in-house planning or project management group: 21 percent of businesses compared to 13 percent of institutions have an in-house architectural staff and more than half of businesses (57 percent) have in-house planning or project management (compared to 32 percent of institutions). Educational service institutions are much more likely to have relied on architects for a variety of services than institutional and medium-sized business professionals.

Institutional respondents place a higher priority on aesthetics and the way a facility fits in with its physical surroundings than do businesses. Nearly three-quarters of healthcare, education, and nonprofit organizations said the design statement of a facility and the way it fits into physical surroundings is a major priority, compared to slightly more than half of business clients.

Institutions are more likely to have a board of trustees, board of directors, or executive board make the final decision regarding an architecture firm. Businesses are more likely to have their president or CEO make this decision.

The functional aspects of a renovation/new construction project are more important than aesthetics

Institutional and business clients alike place a greater value on building functions than on aesthetics. Of the 10 items tested, more than 90 percent of the respondents rated fire- and life-safety systems, air quality, and the efficiency as major priorities. The design statement and way the facility fits in with its physical surroundings were at the bottom of the list.

More than half of all the survey respondents said their company or organization is planning renovation work in the next 18 months, and more than a third said they are planning to undertake new construction projects in the next 18 months.

Compliance with the Americans with Disabilities Act, for instance, is a major concern, and both institutions and business have already made modifications to their facilities. Nearly a third said they have installed ramps, another quarter have made rest-room improvements, and 23 percent have done other types of remodeling or are currently in the process.

The findings of the survey and focus groups suggest a number of marketing implications:

• Because clients tend to think about hiring an architect only to design a specific building project or renovation, architects need to promote and market more aggressively pre-design services like programming and site selection as well as post-design services such as facility management. Instead of marketing services around specific projects, architects might emphasize how they can be valuable in evaluating a client's building needs, choosing a site, and making a building run efficiently once it's completed. Clients don't think of architects as providing these services and, therefore, may turn to other professionals. Making clients aware of these pre- and post-design services can, in turn, lay the groundwork for long-term relationships.

> " *If clients select your firm on your price, they will leave for another firm's* "

- Rather than emphasizing their design capabilities first, architects need to demonstrate their ability to listen and respond to the client's needs, their technical and organizational ability, and their desire to serve the client. While design ability is certainly important, when a client hires an architect, it is the way the architect listens and responds that leads most clients to select one architect over another.

- When it comes to money issues, architects need to demonstrate an ability to manage budgets as well as schedules rather than emphasizing low fees. Fees are considered a relative cost.

- Architects need to disprove the perception that they are arrogant, elitist, and demanding, particularly since clients say responsiveness in an architect is very important to them. If an architect is demanding and not a good listener, a client may be inclined to use an architect only for the most basic of services, turning to others for some pre- and post-design services.

- Marketing approaches should be tailored to the specific needs of the client. As the survey results show, there are some striking differences between institutional and business clients in how they make decisions and what they value in an architect. For example, when marketing to a school system, don't show slides of high-rise buildings without demonstrating how that high-rise experience relates to the proposed educational facility.

- Renovation, as opposed to new construction, continues to provide the greatest number of opportunities for architects. The Americans with Disabilities Act continues

124   to provide business opportunities to architects as clients
work to make their facilities comply.

All in all, it's a good time to be a professional service
provider in this industry. The process of design is to a large
degree appreciated. Designers who understand their
clients' needs and who can negotiate and then deliver value
will prosper in the twenty-first century.

TRUE SUCCESS: ARE YOU MEASURING UP?

"The future of dance? If I knew, I'd want to do it first."

MARTHA GRAHAM

S uccess is not just about talent and speed—it is also much about an organization's operating culture. This point was powerfully brought home from an unlikely source. It's a story worth telling.

Recently, I drove from my office in Atlanta to interview a candidate at Georgia Tech. Not wanting to be late, I took the first available parking spot and headed toward the architecture building where the meeting was to be held. Parking on this campus can be tricky. Feeling relieved for having a parking spot, I realized I was inside a labyrinth of buildings and was uncertain of the shortest route to my destination. I asked a custodian for help.

What I expected was direction. What I got was direction and service. This warm and gracious gentleman said, "come with me, because it's confusing to get there from here." I followed. He took me inside a collegiate hall and down the corridor to an elevator. Following a meandering route, we arrived at an opening where the custodian said to me, "there is the building you are looking for...now you should be able to get to your meeting on time."

And I did, except that, when I arrived, I discovered that the meeting had just been postponed and the school had tried to contact me with the message. The Dean's assistant apologized with much more energy than one would normally expect. Another staff member brought me a soft drink. While I rested and made a few phone calls to adjust

> *Explore toward new edges in civility.*

my schedule, the Dean's assistant came to me and again apologized for the last minute schedule change. I asked her if she had a campus map since I wanted to take the shortest route back to my car. Without hesitation she said, "I'll show you." My protests went unheeded. She walked me outside and then drove me to my car a mile and a half away. Friendly, helpful, caring, and efficient. This was not the Ritz Carlton, I must remind you—but Georgia Tech.

This experience has stuck with me because I learned a lesson on civility that says a lot about this institution's culture. It's much more than teaching, intelligence, technology, and research—it's about human caring and follow-through.

Firms often forget how important the little things are—so much so that they tend to become the big things. It is the actions of people that create what is special and unique about an organization's culture. Culture shapes and gives continuity to success. That is why firms and organizations ask themselves who they really are. What is their work for anyway? And how do their actions reflect the answer to that question?

How different are you? What is your uniqueness—and where does it show up? How do you treat people? How much civility do you exhibit? How human do you sound to your clients, and to your staff? When things go wrong—and they will from time to time, it is too often that the strategies are discussed first. We sometimes strangle strategies to death through analysis, research, discussion and fear. Why not start with discussing culture? It could lead to uncommon levels of service—significant, unique, and perhaps even more relevant than the newest, latest, most innovative strategy. And of course, the positive nature of your culture is one of the most strategic assets an organization can have.

TOWARD PERSONAL
FULFILLMENT

KEVIN ROCHE, FAIA

The city of the past we remember by its handsome surviving fragments; but we do not always consider the social conditions that caused these buildings to be built—even though the literature of the past is replete with vivid descriptions of social injustice.

When looking at the city of the present, we tend to have the same myopic vision—we see the monuments, the tree-lined boulevards, the vibrant avenues; but we do not always see behind those facades the desolation, the hopelessness of so many.

The city is the habitat of the community—the measure of its civilization, the center of its commerce, the spawning ground for its culture.

What, then, are we to think of our cities today? If they are a record of our civilization, what is being said about us? That we are thoughtful planners and good builders? Hardly. That we respect nature and our environment? Hardly.

The litany is long and painful.

What, then, are we saying about ourselves? That we don't care?

Who would wish to have such an epithet?!

Whatever the cities of the future become, the seeds of the future are in our hearts and minds now. What we conceive today is born tomorrow.

The future grows from our reason, from our compassion, from our desire to improve—there is no other source.

Government is blind if we do not give it eyes. It is mute if we do not give it voice. It cannot act if we do not give it will.

It is we who have the responsibility to reason well and to sacrifice.

It is we who have the responsibility to create a habitat that reflects, at last, the aspirations of our democracy.

If we truly believe this—if we act by what we truly believe—then we shall pass on to the next generation the foundations for a better city, a better community, a better world.

"It is clear that there is a great deal to be done by the
architects of the new reality. It is clear that they will be
recruited from those who can perceive the way into
a more enlightened future. What is needed is a state of
mind that is creative rather than destructive. I encourage
us all to study success that leads to greater success
and to make bold initiatives."

JONAS SALK, M.D.

There are more heroes today than at any other time
in our history. You wouldn't know that from the
morning news. The "police blotter" preoccupa-
tion with violence feeds a prevailing Decline-and-Fall tone
that's frankly poisonous. Viewer discretion is most
emphatically advised!

Sometimes it seems as if negativism is worshiped by edi-
torial columnists. Perhaps they want us to think of them as
in-the-know sophisticates. But negativism is a false god that
devours its children: it defeats progress, creates suspicion
and mistrust, and raises what I call the "hassle factor."

Keep your perspective. The September 11th terrorist acts
against the World Trade Center and the Pentagon were
devastating and unprecedented. The loss of human life was
horrific, making the destruction of one of the world's
greatest architectural works an unfortunate sideshow. The
damage to the psyche was also unprecedented for me personally. And yet, life and work goes on.

Nonetheless, on September 11th, I chose not to read newspapers until the end of the day. I chose to embargo the repetitive news. The first ten hours after you get out of bed should be reserved for clear thinking, innovation, and smart work.

News radio, television, and the paper at the beginning of the day sabotage quality of life. They can trouble the human spirit. The daily dose of mayhem and malfeasance is best consumed during non-peak performance time.

A better way to enjoy your morning orange juice and get your own creative juices flowing is to set your daily goals or reflect on those exceptional men and women who have and are making a difference. With little effort, you can find heroes and mentors everywhere, especially in the face of uncertainty and fear.

> *The daily dose of mayhem and malfeasance is best consumed during non-peak performance time.*

At this moment, I'm thinking of George White, former Architect of the Capitol, who is an inspired steward of our heritage; Ambassador Richard Swett, a powerful advocate for design leadership; Louis Harris, pollster, who gives democracy a voice; Norman Koonce, former president of The American Architectural Foundation and an architect committed a public understanding of and participation in shaping environments through design.

In moments of reflection and solitude, I think of another of my heroes, Dr. Jonas Salk, who makes the point succinctly: "Study success and we will see ways to create new success!"

I can't think of a better breakfast for champions.

CONFIDENCE AND COMPETENCE

"When I was twelve years old and had decided to become an architect, my parents had the good grace not to mention that the field did not have many women, and even put me in touch with architect Louise Hall."

ORTRUDE B. WHITE, FAIA

Clients are not looking for architects who pressure the design process with a peacock display of ego or, more troublesome, jerk around the design team. Instead, they're in the market for professionals who know their own strengths and deliver the goods with full confidence.

This is to say, confidence like competence belongs as much to the repertoire of a successful designer as it does to a winning athlete. Neither competence not confidence comes naturally; we're all born reluctantly and innocent of skills into a pretty intimidating world. But over time competence can be earned and confidence learned.

Schools of architecture do just fine in transmitting the art and science that are the heritage of design. However, most do not teach courses in leadership and entrepreneurship. That's unfortunate for many reasons, but most importantly because this is precisely the training that nurtures the articulateness and poise that are the winning attributes of confidence. Without that confidence, the competence the architect brings to the bargaining table simply does not shine.

Fortunately, professional development is an ongoing opportunity at all stages of a professional's life. The art of confidence building is no exception. There are many good resources available to the designer as near at hand as the closest bookstore. I always highly recommend a couple of small but powerful books by Max DePree—*Leadership is an Art* and *Leadership Jazz*. A chapter at breakfast or just before bed is more than enough to provide the minimum daily requirement of valuable insights. Socrates said, "The greatest way to live with honor in this world is to be what we pretend to be."

With self training and on-the-job experience, confidence grows; when leavened with honesty, competence will be recognized and rewarded.

LEADERS MANAGE
THEIR TIME

"There's more to life than merely increasing its speed."

GANDHI

Voluntary involvement in the life of a profession is its greatest resource. We all know that. And there's hardly one of us who wouldn't get in line to sign up. Right? But not right now.

Who has the time? We're already pulled in all directions trying to juggle the demands of making a living. So if you catch me next week, perhaps I can pencil in a couple of hours. But I'm not promising anything.

Sound familiar?

Is your schedule really full?

There's the story of an exceptionally effective consultant and speaker who had great success in getting even the busiest folks to volunteer their time. This is how he'd do it.

He would stand holding an empty box before his audience of high-powered and high-pressured executives. Then he would open package after package of billiard balls and drop them into the box until the tops of the balls peeked over the edge.

At this point he would say to his audience, "Is it full?"

To their eyes, it clearly was. Then he opened package after package of marbles and poured them in. Of course, they dropped down through the crevices left by the billiard balls. When not a single additional marble would fit in, he said, "Now is it full?" Before anyone could answer, he opened bags of BB's and poured bag after bag into that box.

When the BB's came up to the rim, he said, "What do you think?" By this time, his audience had developed a healthy reluctance to jump to the obvious incorrect conclusion. So he rewarded their dawning insight by pouring a bucket of sand into the box. The sand sifted down through all the spaces until it looked as if the box were at last full.

But then he said, "It's still not really full." And with that, he poured a bucket of water into that box, and still the box did not overflow.

Leaders know how to set priorities

If we're really honest with ourselves, we know we can always find the time to do what we believe is important. The sticking point is not a matter of scheduling; it all comes down to priorities.

When it comes to setting priorities, this is what I've found works for me: list all the activities competing for my time. Then, write down personal goals and values. With the second list as a kind of template, I'm able to schedule how I spend my time.

If a commitment to your profession is not part of your values and goals, your schedule will always be too full. But if the commitment is there, you'll find the time. And you will make a difference.

YOU ARE IN THE DRIVER'S SEAT

"The trouble in life, in business as well as sports, is that too many people are afraid of competition. The result is that, in some circles, people have come to sneer at success if it costs hard work, training, and sacrifice."

KNUTE ROCKNE

Each designer has the right to belong to a professional organization. But to hear some talk, "right" is not the word uppermost in their minds. The way they describe it, you would think membership was a necessary evil or beneath them. What difference does it make in any case, they shrug, whether or not they get involved?

Design professionals who talk this way are acting like the health of the organization that represents their best interests has little if anything to do with the future of their practice. To make the divorce complete, they back away from active involvement.

Apathy is a disease. It seeks out those who are self-centered and have closed minds. It strikes those who don't care about the future. Worse, it cripples the efforts of those who do.

Go to the upcoming meetings where your officers are chosen. How many candidates are running? What percentage of the membership is in the room? More to the point, who's setting the goals?

Most frustrating for those who really care about their profession, it's sometimes the members on the sidelines who shape everyone else's future. After all, they're typically the largest voting block!

Their decision to sit on their hands when it comes to the regulatory climate shaping their profession or the documents guiding it or the public appreciation and understanding of their work—all this, and much more, means buying into the prevailing agenda whatever it might be. Look, Ma, no hands, and yet their disengagement sets their profession's priorities!

The collective voice speaks loudest

There are at least two problems in letting a silent majority call the shots. Although they acquiesce to an agenda or a style of leadership, they won't accept responsibility for the results. Instead, the buck typically stops at someone else's door—the large firms, the small firms, the old boys, the staff.

If you're in a position of leadership, pulling out the barbs of unfair criticism from the very people you try to serve is painful enough. Yet it doesn't begin to compare to the pain of opportunities lost. Think of the ideas never brought to light, the creative energy untapped, and the initiatives left unbegun because the full creativity of your profession is not turned on.

> *Cynicism is a disease in firm management and apathy cripples the efforts of those who care about the future.*

There's something else: A collective voice—whether it's a professional organization or an entire nation—speaks most persuasively when it comes from an organization actively united behind a compelling vision. That's being "member driven" in the best sense.

If you're an architect, upgrade your credentials. If you're in another design profession, seek out the best fit and make a commitment to share your dreams and help energize new policies and actions. Your profession's future in no small way needs you to do this.

"Networking works to the degree of your network."

ANNE BOWE

I recall being in the office-studio of one of New York's most famous architects when he challenged his younger colleagues to associate with the right people. He was talking about powerful personalities. But he had in mind something far more lasting than the rich and famous.

He was reflecting on architectural education, in particular the very critical, often negative, feedback students get when a jury reviews projects. Although he had no quarrel with the kind of clear-eyed probing that challenges a student's assumptions and provokes them to stretch their perceptions of the possible, he was troubled by the slash and burn tactics of many a critique. He made the point that young, impressionable designers hear criticisms more deeply than they hear compliments.

Many of us, whatever our age, remember negative comments far longer than positive feedback. A strong, relentless diet of "put downs" is less likely to build muscle than it is to wound the spirit of a young talent just trying out its wings.

Celebrate your inner strength

What is the secret of those whose spirits aren't broken? They refuse to be the victims of poisonous cynicism. They

142   somehow reach into themselves or are encouraged by a selfless mentor to understand and celebrate their unique strengths. Knowing that they have chosen the best, most exciting career available, they seek out the company of those who breathe the same positive, "can do" air.

That doesn't mean turning a deaf ear to the critical opinions of others. Thoughtful feedback is the breakfast of champions. However, a steady diet of gratuitous slam dunks can also lead to a lifestyle of accepting limitations that others would impose on us. I tell my sons to hang around friends who are positive, friends who challenge them to run faster, jump higher, and learn more. Spend your time with people you want to emulate for their accomplishments, not those you feel superior to. Those are the kind of people who take joy in your growth.

[handwritten margin note: time to change when this happens]

My New York City architect friend was urging the young members of his firm to seek out quality, successful people who know how to achieve, people who don't envy or begrudge your gifts but who value you precisely for your strengths.

Use the critical eye to grow

There's someone else—the person who looks back at you every morning when you stand before the mirror. Is that person eager to think about your worth? Is there a deep appreciation for the value of your unique gifts? Is there an honest recognition of your strengths *[handwritten: and weaknesses]* and a commitment to build on them?

Use the critical eye that stares back at you for positive development—not for limiting growth. Use the critical eye

for developing stronger plans, not for defeating them
whether those plans come from a colleague or are your own. If that's the way your inner voice is talking to you, you're in good company.

A CASE OF INDIGESTION

"Example is not the main thing in influencing others.
It is the only thing."

ALBERT SCHWEITZER

I t's almost noon, but I haven't gotten over last night's dinner. The food was good. Still, I came away with a bad taste I can't shake.

Dinner was a familiar Washington occasion—a mix of bankers, lawyers, business people, and architects. We talked about the economy in general and commerce and industry in particular. I picked up some good insights about where we seem to be heading—even a bit of cautious optimism.

But we were served a plateful of static, and it came from architects. From the opening basket of bread to the second cup of decaf, the architects at my table seemed caught up in a contest to see who could bad-mouth their profession the most.

> **Architects and designers must be the first and the most insistent in making their own case.**

This was not the familiar architect "A" criticizing the designs of architect "B". This was open season on what was being described as the heartbreak of practice. Those who were complaining the loudest saw no future in architecture.

Imagine what the business owners were thinking. I know architects around the country who would have flagged deep pockets and projects waiting to be born.

But these architects saw none of that. Although they were seated with potential clients, not one was making a case for problem solving, much less vision. To a client's ear, the prospect of working with any one of them sounded like a sure-fire ticket to trouble.

Without denying that architects should be fairly compensated for the real value they bring to a project, and without glossing over the stress of a profession being dramatically transformed, why weren't they communicating the strengths of their profession? No profession is more deserving of the public's respect and a client's appreciation. But architects must be the first and most insistent in making their own case. And no first step is more important than believing in yourself and your profession.

Coming off like a winner is no guarantee you'll win the contract every time. Negativism, on the other hand, is a self-fulfilling prophecy.

INNOVATION AND INTEGRITY: THERE IS NO AGE LIMIT

EXCERPTS FROM A COMMENCEMENT ADDRESS DELIVERED AT THE UNIVERSITY OF MINNESOTA

I was a student at the University of Minnesota and taught some classes here as well. The sense of learning and gaining an understanding of people and community as well as opportunity and responsibility—has enriched me beyond what I could have hoped for. This school has given me both challenge and support. It has inspired me to dream about new realities and continues to provide in my soul a source of valuable perspective.

I think about the University of Minnesota often. I encourage each of you to support higher education more actively and to get a little sentimental about your school once in awhile. Nothing great is ever achieved without enthusiasm and no university achieves greatness or sustains it without enthusiastic support. Alumni, faculty, and community really do make a quantum difference.

Knowing something about the strength in today's young, aspiring designers, I encourage you to put your university on your list of lifetime priorities. Wonderful results will follow.

In 1978 a search committee of architects headed by Ed Sovik of SMSQ and David Hall of Ellerbe Becket made a recommendation to then president Ken Skold that I be named the executive vice president of the Minnesota Society of Architects. Their action and my subsequent involvement has changed my life more than I could have imagined. It has been magical.

There are, of course, disappointments. For example, I continue to be dismayed when politicians strive for and even celebrate not what works, but what wins. Not what seems prudent for the long term, but whether it is immediately useful and, if so, how.

In his book *Hard Thinking*, Herb Meyer writes: "While politics will certainly attract good people, it will also attract bad people—people who will lower standards rather than uphold them. And declining standards, as you know, have a momentum all their own; the more they decline, the more they decline. At first the good people are the ones who raise standards. They are the ones who struggle to maintain standards. Finally, they are the ones whose standards are merely declining more slowly than everyone else."

This is a problem relevant to each of us here today because organizations, institutions, and levels of government have the potential to slip from a culture that is both solid and visionary to one that is soft and filled with paralysis and psychobabble.

I recommend you get involved like architect, Congressman and Ambassador Richard Swett and urban planner and Congressman Doug Bereuter. A lot depends on good people. The definition of politics doesn't have to slide.

Let me be blunt about another troubling development: I've also been disappointed with the media. We are in what is being characterized as the information age, but just how is this information helping us toward civility and progress?

Newspapers, magazines, and the electronic media are bombarding us with messages, many of which are negative. This, then, brings its own disorientation and a national confusion from being unable to see any problem clearly. There's an information fog.

This week's *Barron's* speaks to the disappointment: "The information gutter has far outstripped the much ballyhooed information highway in both development and traffic."

Another disappointment and one that I have testified on before Congress is the gradual uglification of America. You know what I'm talking about, and I ask each of you to join with me to advocate good design and environmental protection.

Inside each of you is a unique and very special talent. Not only are you motivated to be successful, but clearly the world needs designers to be successful in exercising to the fullest their special talent.

While we have problems to confront, keep your perspective and keep in mind that you have these special innate gifts as well as a good education. The strength of our future lies with you. Not people riding out a term, but people actively seeking wisdom. Not people of despair and cynicism, but people filled with hope. Not people who see this educational experience as an end in and of itself, but people searching to grow new skills and always seeking new knowledge.

You know that successful people are not just lucky. Good things happen because people are willing to think smart, work hard, make some sacrifices, and take risks. So be resilient under stress. And keep up the sense of humor even when you face days of disappointment. Our culture is evolving and you're going to be playing an increasingly significant role.

In this time of human evolution and change, it will be up to each of us to be energized rather than swept away from the swift current of change. John K. Galbraith has written: "Faced with the prospect of change or proving that no change is necessary, most people get on with finding the proof." Hubert Humphrey casts the challenge we all face in a more positive light: "The rocks across the stream of change may be slippery, but they're there to help you get to the other side."

On the other side, I see today's design graduates at the center of relevancy and value. Not just players, but leaders and innovators. Not just looking at the current landscape of problems, but transcending them to see ahead to a new map of opportunity. Not just marginally compensated, but fully and fairly rewarded for their knowledge and creativity. Not just concerned about design and the environment, but passionate about design and the environment. Not just compromising during political and organizational confrontation, but with courageous insight offering ideas and inspiration to raise standards.

But the hour grows late and you have a whole new world to master and redeem. So, as the stewardship of this planet is increasingly entrusted to your hands, keep these three things in mind; recite them, if you will, like a mantra:

1. You have wisely selected a career in architecture, planning, and design!
2. This is a time of great opportunity for people with your talent and intelligence!
3. Nothing is impossible!

Now, instead of worrying about the future, go out and create it.

A TURNING POINT IN THE HISTORY OF THE PROFESSION

"Now we ask: Is there a point at which the principle of change will be fused with the principle of permanence?...a perpetual re-beginning and a continual return."

OCTAVIO PAZ

It will take time to change the attitudinal and scientific culture of the design professions. As Thomas Kuhn observes in his seminal work *The Structure of Scientific Revolutions*, when a paradigm starts to shift, those wedded to the outgoing paradigm tend to resist. Herbert E. Meyer reminds us that "in the end they are defeated rather than persuaded; they are pushed aside to make room for new people who are more comfortable with the new perception and more fluent in the various subtleties."

What about those designers who, by contrast, understand how to fit in and capitalize on the new playing fields? They have successfully evolved. They are open to more evolution. They are resilient and often in their own quiet way are gaining increasing confidence and optimism about the future. What they are doing may be very quiet most of the time. But make no mistake: They are revolutionizing the design professions. They are redefining their professions for the better.

Based on what I have seen in looking at a number of success stories, there are five principles driving those participating in and benefiting from this model:

1. No one owes you anything—not the state registration laws, not the government, not the economy, not your employer, not your parents. You must invent your own sustainable future and be an *entrepreneur* of your life.

2. Chaos and change are a major force in a designer's life. Love it or hate it, but don't whine. *Take advantage of the infinite possibilities* now available to you in a world of constant flow.

3. Design your life to be lean and results oriented. *Follow your values and your vision.* Your values will give you integrity and peace; your vision will energize and propel you ahead to achieve your goals.

4. Only you can make personal and professional choices. These principles will support you:
   - Be focused as you take action; know your priorities.
   - Have a strong will and positive commitment.
   - Be anticipatory and resilient.

5. Take care of your *relationships* and leverage your experience and wisdom. Leave a legacy that makes a difference.

Taken together these five rules of design enterprise are not by themselves a recipe for inevitable success: they seem, however, to be the key principles guiding today's and tomorrow's designers toward careers that are personally rewarding and professionally fulfilling. In the brave new world opening before us, they are the gateway that empowers designers to make a profound contribution to the quality of life. And with that contribution will come renewed respect for those who, along with nature, shape our world.

THE ASCENDENT DESIGNER

156

TRANSFORMING
PROFESSIONAL LIFE

"The fact that the designs of nature and the designs of man
can be analyzed according to a common set of criteria
stems from the fact that they have a basic property in
common: they are solutions to a problem.
Some of the most important designs are just as much
problem statements as they are solutions. The problem
can come first but often it is more complex than that.
Revealing the problem is part of the solution."

JANS BERNSEN

The pace of change is exponentially faster than it has ever been. The design professions are experiencing not only linear innovation—that which you might plan for—but non-linear and unexpected changes. That's why I say: Don't just plan—invent. Put in place a process that develops both your future vision and a sustainable business model.

Responsiveness to change is a key component of today's healthy designer. As a principal of one firm said to me: "To dawdle is to die." When architects and other design professionals all sell the same thing, and when services are delivered the same way, it is the organizational equivalent of inbreeding.

It doesn't take long for clients to recognize when services go stale or become irrelevant compared to the other choices in the market. Clients aren't just looking at licensed architects, engineers, and interior designers but a full range of choices and competitors that are challenging the traditional role of the design professional.

Ideas mutate in nature and as well in design. Right now, some designers and the firms they work in are experiencing more inertia than evolution. These firms are finding it difficult to renew themselves. As a result, some of them are dying. Most often, employees see and understand the decline long before the partners do.

Is it too radical to say that the industry is in a revolution? The answer is no. Radical change is with us and, for many, it is out ahead of us as well. In the design professions, to be ahead of the curve is rare.

There are important questions to anticipate—and answer. What will be fundamentally different —and what could still be the same? Does digital potential strengthen or weaken the architect in the future? Does the potential of e-business solutions strengthen design firm...or obliterate them? What does the relevant firm of today do to sustain and strengthen its position? Must you stay on the cutting edge or die? Where is the cutting edge anyway? And is there a way to win in commodity priced services?

> **" Ideas mutate in nature and as well in the business of design. "**

As I hope you have come to understand, architects and designers can actually create the future. Since, as we have discussed, worry is a misuse of the imagination. Instead, you should be motivated to intercept the future—and make it a better one.

Best practice

A commodity market is one where the key variable is price. Yes, it's entirely possible to run a profitable firm as a commodity—take those firms that specialize in the roll-out of retail chain stores, for example. However, many firms tell me that it often isn't as rewarding—and some say it's just not as much fun.

That doesn't mean design firms shouldn't think like companies that sell commodities. Lowering costs by bundling products with services and creating new levels of efficiency can make architects and designers more competitive in the larger market. We call this best practice, and it involves not only smart design management but a nurturing corporate environment, strong marketing and branding, and innovative thinking to capture future potential.

While all firms are different, best practice firms all share the following attributes, and yours can too:

- You will hire, train, and keep capable people.
- You will find profitable markets.
- You will select clients with great care.
- You will display strong communication skills internally and externally.
- You will nurture innovation.
- You will achieve or beat profit goals.
- You will address growth in both quality and quantity of work.
- You will know the risks and protect against them.
- You will plan for leadership and ownership transitions.

Perhaps you actually work for or are running a best practice firm. If that is the case, you likely also know that,

best practices

while you can't predict the future, it's worthwhile to study
trends and anticipate possible scenarios.

Every design firm either has competitive fitness or they don't. Each day firms either get stronger or weaker—more relevant or less. Many aren't taking advantage of their opportunities. Or, in the words of one client: "These people are so busy catching up that they don't take time to understand their future potential."

THE ASCENDENT DESIGNER

A new industry is being created. It will be defined not only by government regulations, but by business interests, safety issues, and concerns about quality of life and the natural environment. It will be led by innovation in practice management, leadership, and design creativity.

This new industry will be created by those who take responsibility and are willing to be held accountable for it. There are individuals and firms who are designing and building a very different future. There are architects who "talk rather than do" and those who, when given a choice between a future they've deliberately built and a future that they've fallen into, opt for the passive model. But among many there is an understanding that we have not only entered a new century—we have entered a new industry, one that has more in common with aviation and technology than with the tarnished construction industry of the previous century.

Let's look at what we might call "the ascendant designer"—the designer who is relevant and successfully changing in surprising, and sometimes contradictory, ways to gain success and win attention. These are the individuals and firms who are capturing new value from their services. They differ dramatically from those who are leaking value by not recognizing opportunities to close the gap between their core competencies, their services and their clients' needs.

What are the areas that ascendant architects anticipate?

Design information flows

Everyone is in the information business. If you think about it, it has always been this way. Think back to the Gothic cathedral. Information did not come to people—people had to go to information. Today we have broadband Internet connectivity. Digital networks make it possible to link rich information to people wherever they are. But the concept is the same: information is not only critical, it's essential—and the means of transmitting it is at the center of our civilization.

> *Fresh information is not only critical—it is essential for growth and success.*

The architecture business will be substantially affected by the shifting economics of information because information is a component of value in the design firm.

The Internet's power lies in its ubiquity and simplicity. It has the ability to permeate and catalyze our economy in a manner comparable to the interstate highway system. To a casual observer, it may appear the Internet is receding in importance. In reality, the next net platforms and hi-tech solutions are bulking up in preparation for the next big wave of growth. Firms must not only plan for new information systems in their current projects, but they must think about the future design of these information platforms—and have a hand in shaping them.

They must also seize the enterprise advantage of advanced information systems in their practices. Can you afford to be left behind?

The technological world

Technology may become more invisible and more taken for granted but it will annihilate traditional industry practices. There will be a seamless continuum between conceiving forms and implementing them. I recently visited the Frank Gehry Café in New York City. Nothing in that space would be possible without the technology of Catia®—the program used to design the Boeing 777 and the PT Cruiser.

Is Catia® the last innovation in design technology? Is it as far as design tools will ever progress?

Of course not. Design processes migrated forward from 2-D forward to 3-D and then 4-D. Soon there will be real time feedback from every stroke of the pen. We should not fool ourselves into thinking that the end of technological breakthroughs is in sight. Instead, the horizons are expanding—and new threats and opportunities will be of a breakaway nature.

The pre-assembled solution

Soon building solutions will be pre-assembled on a large scale. Owners and manufacturers will create powerful alliances, eliminating many process steps. There will be

162 fewer people needed—and there will be diminished labor requirements thanks to robotics and efficient systems.

Even now, clients can get customized pre-fabricated projects that almost appear like one-off buildings. Author Joe Pine calls this "mass customization." Arthur Gensler and Tom Pfeiffer call it "smart business." At *www.work stage.com*, you'll see how an alliance is creating buildings that are mass-produced and yet individual to each user.

Eventually, high-end design solutions could be pre-assembled, and Pritzker Prize-winning architects could design even inexpensive building types like those chain motels that surround local airports.

Coordinating for efficiency

In a few years, building construction will be 20 to 40 percent more efficient. Better information and technical coordination is the best opportunity for value enhancement and greater efficiency. We are moving from fragmentation to united solutions. You used to have to buy twelve pieces of office equipment to have a home office; now you can just go to Kinko's. Design processes will soon be integrated in a similar manner.

Advanced integration will be highly valued. In five years, integrated delivery will become nearly 60 percent of all project delivery, as opposed to less than 30 percent today. Traditional and design-bid-build projects will decline by half, from 59 percent today to approximately 30 percent. With the convergence of design and construction, it stands to reason that firms with the best business skills and design talent will have the competitive advantage.

Designer buildings will become more in demand and more common. There is a new point of intersection between popular and professional taste—we have entered a period where it seems that everyone wants good design. This phenomenon is hurting American architects who haven't yet risen to "superstar" status. Go from city to city and European and Asians are taking the lead on design innovation. This isn't a problem, it's an opportunity.

We are also moving from elite to universal. A few years ago, a color printer cost $10,000; today they cost one-twentieth of that. Likewise, signature designer buildings are not just for patron clients anymore. And the potential for profit is enormous. Not only does Michael Graves get a premium fee to design a building, he captures a royalty on each sale of his patented product designs.

THE NEXT DESIGN PROFESSIONS

Real innovation in design happens in context. That context requires highly collaborative processes. The myth of a split between designers and contractors is becoming a charming artifact of the past. Where there is obvious binary opposition in this industry, there is also the greatest opportunity for breakaway new value propositions. Take a counter position to conventional wisdom and you're likely to be onto something that offers new and fresh value.

This industry convergence is prompted by efficiency and motivated by quality. Take a moment next time you are on the Internet and check out the Web sites of four contractors held in high repute and four best-of-class architecture firms. Go, for instance, to Haskell, Gensler, Tishman, HGA, Opus, RTKL, Beck, and NBBJ. These firms have established reputations in either design or construction, but if you go to their Web sites you can't immediately tell which is a construction company and which the design firm.

In the next phase of design value migration, typical commercial projects could be delivered in half the time. Currently, 20 percent of total delivery time on a typical office building is in design. This, some say, can be reduced by 60 percent. It is becoming somewhat of a myth that good design takes a long time. It was once true—but the time required to design projects is shrinking. If it's not you who is taking less time to do this work then someone else is creating both great design and quality—all at a speed that was unthinkable only a few years ago.

> **This new convergence is prompted by efficiency and motivated by quality.**

The best of two worlds

The current trend is toward full service and smaller niche firms. Take The Beck Group on the one hand, and Glenn Murcutt on the other.

Beck—just named by *Fortune* magazine as one of the best employers in the world today—is a full service real estate organization that provides financing, pre-design consulting, design and architecture, construction services and post design services all in an integrated neo-design-build model.

With Glenn Murcutt (who has won the Thomas Jefferson Award at the University of Virginia and the top architecture awards in both Denmark and Australia), we see how an architect, operating out of his house in Australia, can gain international attention while doing great design—and charging a 12 percent flat fee. He has no staff and prefers to supervise construction on each of his form-giving projects—many in the outback of Australia. Is he successful? You can count the ways simply by watching him smile as he talks about his clients and his work.

Architects and designers must choose between these and other attractive extremes. It is the only way to stay responsive to clients and personal goals. Chose a niche and excel in it. Your small size will give you great flexibility. Or integrate across a broad range of products and services. Your reach will allow you to meet future expectations, even if they are radically different than the expectations of today.

There will be radical new value propositions in design and construction—new processes, new technologies, new business models, new strategies. There will be new efficiencies—and new competitors. Clients will expect more, often for less.

There is nothing wrong with creating a niche and sticking with it. This can be smart enterprise. The industry leaders of tomorrow, however, will be those who reach for more. Alliances are often the solution.

The power of alliance

The word alliance was first used in the English language in the fourteenth century. Simply put, the meaning is "a state of union or combination; the act of uniting" or "to form a combination for a common objective."

You have no doubt heard of alliances such as the Global Design Alliance, which now numbers almost fifteen firms. GDA's combined brainpower gives clients seeking expertise and value a network of options, and creates a system where innovative, breakaway ideas get shared. Consider also the new alliance between Callison Architects; Wimberly Allison Tong & Goo; and Thompson, Ventulett, Stainback & Associates. Here we see the specialties of retail, hospitality and hotel design and convention centers converging into an alliance for better marketplace positioning, communication, and service delivery.

Alliances enable firms to address the following practice trends:

- Embrace change
- Provide solutions, not just designs
- Utilize strategic and project alliances to deliver value
- Commit to technology
- Make speed a reality
- Find new ways to get attention in the information economy
- Be an expert in the business of their clients

Alliances have become popular because they help firms position themselves for success. Firms enter into alliances for the following reasons:

alliances & teammaking

- To capitalize on their core competencies
- To turn their weaknesses into positive competitive strengths via the alliance team

- To become more performance conscious
- To generate greater success in highly complex situations
- To increase both depth and confidence in the work of the team
- To position themselves as a clear expert leader anticipatory of the clients needs, wants, and expectations

Alliances can be quick, lively, responsive—that which we call alacrity. The combination of talents can create an eager willingness and readiness for the future. We look for the word align in alliance. Align is the action of bringing two or more firms into a particular policy or power structure.

At the opposite end of alliance is alienation: a process whereby firms become progressively estranged from central aspects of an objective. As many firms have discovered, alliances do not always work out. They can be exploitative, contradictory and antagonistic. Competition and self-interest can eclipse community and cooperation.

An alliance always has the potential to alienate. Someone or some company will spin outside the alliance by choice or they will become the weak link in the team. But the momentum and alacrity of the alliance wave will build strength as long as it aligns with the needs of client audiences and prevailing economic conditions. Alliances need strong leadership just as sports teams need good coaches and orchestras need experienced conductors.

Whether in an alliance or a niche firm, leaders set the agenda and the tone of the work. They shape the policy, and create the world of tomorrow.

The architecture and design professions are changing rapidly. They are under attack from other service providers. Designers are often confused about long-term goals. But the future is also brimming with opportunity. A new successful approach is unfolding:

- Develop a coherent, positive point of view. No architects or designers outperform their own aspirations. Your point of view should be expansive and motivating.
- Create a vision and a plan. Think non-linearly about futures invention. Your action plan should be edgy, not just last year's success formula.
- Pursue a coalition or alliance to deliver stronger solutions.
- Extinguish inertia. That is to say, co-opt and neutralize the anti-change forces around you.
- Use a vocabulary of action and motivation. Don't worry about problems; take advantage of the opportunity to think in new ways. Don't acknowledge binary opposites; build bridges using unifying business logic.
- Renew your goals and consistently achieve them.

If you want to change anything major, you have to do it with other people. Listen. Learn. Teach. Lead. Where does it begin? It begins with an idea, a point of view, and you. This is the design plus enterprise model, and its purpose is to create a new ascendancy in the design professions.

BOOKS

Abramowitz, Ava J., *The Architect's Essentials of Contract Negotiation*, (McGraw-Hill) 2002.

Barker, Joel, *Future Edge*, (William Morrow & Co.) 1992

Bennis, Warren, *On Becoming a Leader*, (Addison-Wesley) 1989.

Brown, John Seely and Paul Duguid, *The Social Life of Information*, (Harvard Business School Press) 2001.

Christensen, Clayton M., *The Innovator's Dilemma: When New Technologies Cause Great Firms to Fail*, (Harvard Business School Press) 1997.

Coleman, Cindy, *Interior Design Handbook of Professional Practice*, (McGraw-Hill) 2001.

Collins, James C. and Jerry I. Porras, *Built to Last: Successful Habits of Visionary Companies*, (HarperCollins) 1994.

Collins, Jim, *Good to Great: Why Some Companies Make the Leap...and Others Don't*, (HarperCollins) 2001.

Covey, Stephen R., *Principle Centered Leadership*, (Summit Books) 1991.

Cramer, James P., *Almanac of Architecture & Design*, (Greenway) 2000-2002.

172 Cramer, James P. and Scott Simpson., *How Firms Succeed: A Field Guide to Design Management*, (Greenway) 2002.

DePree, Max, *Leadership Is an Art*, (Doubleday) 1989.

Drucker, Peter F., *Innovation and Entrepreneurship: Practice and Principles*, (Perennial/Harper & Row) 1985.

Drucker, Peter F., *The Changing World of the Executive*, (Times Books) 1992.

Farson, Richard, *Management of the Absurd: Paradoxes in Leadership*, (Simon & Schuster) 1996.

Flynn-Heapes, Ellen, *Creating Wealth: Principles and Practices for Design Firms*, (SPARKS, The Center for Strategic Planning) 2000.

Friedman, Thomas L., *The Lexus and the Olive Tree: Understanding Globalization*, (Farrar, Straus & Giroux) 1999.

Gad, Thomas, *4-D Branding: Cracking the Corporate Code of the Network Economy*, (Financial Times/Prentice Hall) 2001.

Graham, Katharine, *Personal History*, (Alfred A. Knopf) 1997.

Hart, Susannah and John Murphy, eds., *Brands: The New Wealth Creators*, (New York University Press) 1998.

Kaplan, Robert S. and David P. Norton, *The Strategy-Focused Organization: How Balanced Scorecard Companies Thrive in the New Business Environment*, (Harvard Business School Press) 2000.

Kelley, Tom, *The Art of Innovation: Lessons in Creativity from IDEO, America's Leading Design Firm*, (Doubleday) 2001.

Maister, David H., Charles H. Green, Robert M. Galford, *The Trusted Advisor*, (The Free Press) 2000.

Mau, Bruce, *Life Style*, (Phaidon) 2000.

Mitroff, Ian I., *Smart Thinking for Crazy Times: The Art of Solving the Right Problems*, (Berrett-Koehler Publishers) 1998.

Paz, Octavio, *The Other Voice*, (Harcourt Brace Jovanich) 1990.

Pine II, B. Joseph and James H. Gilmore, *The Experience Economy: Work Is Theatre & Every Business a Stage*, (Harvard Business School Press) 1999.

Rackham, Neil and John DeVincentis, *Rethinking the Sales Force: Redefining Selling to Create and Capture Customer Value*, (McGraw-Hill) 1999.

Schwartz, Peter, Peter Leyden, and Joel Hyatt, *The Long Boom: A Vision for the Coming Age of Prosperity*, (Perseus) 1999.

Schwartz, Peter, *The Art of the Long View*, (Doubleday Currency) 1991.

The American Institute of Architects, *The Architect's Handbook of Professional Practice* (John Wiley & Sons) 2001.

Townsend, Robert, *Up the Organization, How to Stop the Corporation from Stifling People and Strangling Profits*, (Alfred A. Knopf Inc.) 1970.

174 von Ghyczy, Tiha, Bolko von Oetinger, and Christopher Bassford, eds., *Clausewitz on Strategy: Inspiration and Insight from a Master Strategist*, (John Wiley & Sons) 2001.

von Oech, Roger, *Creative Whack Pack*, (U.S. Games) 1992.

Waldrop, M. Mitchell, *Complexity: The Emerging Science at the Edge of Order and Chaos*, (Touchstone) 1992.

JOURNALS/NEWSLETTERS

DesignIntelligence
Monthly newsletter on changes, strategies and trends published by the Design Futures Council.
www.di.net

Harvard Business Review
Monthly journal of the Harvard Business School.
www.hbsp.harvard.edu/hbr/

Strategy + Business
Quarterly journal published by Booz-Allen & Hamilton Inc.
www.strategy-business.com

ACKNOWLEDGEMENTS

This book comes from an assembly of thoughts collected over the years and filed under the name "A New Reality for Architects?" I was often moved by the stories told to me by people in the process of learning valuable lessons from their real world experiences. The joy and the pain all came through.

This file includes stories given me by some who had just experienced bankruptcy and others who had quietly closed their firms. Dreams were interrupted. A new level of insecurity enveloped their lives. I wish to thank and acknowledge, first, those who took the time to share their failures. You will never be forgotten.

Creating a book is a team process. Many people are mentioned and quoted throughout this book. They gave so generously of themselves, and many bared their souls.

I cannot begin to thank the staff of The American Institute of Architects for all they have done to help me with this book. I would also like to express deep gratitude to the staff at Greenway Group and Greenway Consulting.

On a personal level I wish to thank especially Robert Angle, Dean James Barker (now president of Clemson), Diane Barnes, LeRoy Bean, Kirk Blunck, Friedl Bohm, Carol Anne Bundy, Hon. Henry Cisneros, Leo A. Daly III, Dr. Nancy Davis, Richard Farson, Sir Norman Foster, Dean Harrison Fraker, Steve Fiskum, Dean John Gaunt,

Francis Halsband, Beverly Hauschild, Val Hawes, Jerry Hobbs, Bernard Jacob, Dr. Dan Jordan, Robert Kapsch, Duane Kell, Roger Kennedy, Ed Kodet, Gene Kohn, Norman Koonce, Rod Kruse, Dr. Mina Marefat, Charles W. Moore, Bob Mutchler, Leonard Parker, Bill Pederson, Peter Piven, Luke Ives Pontifell, Boone Powell, Rev. Ron Prasek, Peter Rand, Ralph Rapson, Robert Rietow, Kevin Roche, Dr. Jonas Salk, Robert Schwartz, Rex Scouten, Scott Simpson, Rev. John Sonnenday, Ed Sovik, James Stageberg, Hon. Richard Swett, April Thornton, Tom VanHousen, Dean Cynthia Weese, Gary Wheeler, and Hon. George White. Their observations on design, health, wisdom, spiritual strength, and evolution have taught me much that I believe is applicable to architects preparing for the twenty-first century. Bill Caudill was one of my mentors, and I will always be guided by his ideas and beliefs.

My friends at the American Design Council, the Union of International Architects, the Japan Institute of Architects, the Royal Institute of British Architects, The National Building Museum, The Octagon Museum, the Society of Architectural Historians, and Architecture magazine have provided valuable insight and support.

Some of the text in the book comes from presentations and lectures I gave at the University of Minnesota, Clemson University, MIT, the University of Nebraska, the University of Pisa (Italy) and the University of Hawaii-Manoa.

The Council of Architectural Component Executives has many exceptionally dedicated and talented people. I have been greatly enriched through my association with these special people.

Officers of The American Institute of Architects and other leaders of the profession typically give so much of themselves and often are inspirations pushing the profession to new heights. I am especially appreciative of the leadership of the following for helping me conceptually with the content of the book: Harold Adams, Walter Blackburn, Mike Bolinger, Ben Brewer, Bob Broshar, John Busby, Bill Chapin, Syl Damianos, Phil Dinsmore, Joe Esherick, Tom Eyerman, Win Faulkner, Don Hackl, Ernie Hara, George Hartman, Billy Herron, Hugh Newell Jacobsen, Fay Jones, Raj Barr Kumar, Bill Lacy, Jim Lawler, Robert Lawrence, Larry Lies, Louis Marines, Susan Maxman, Richard Meier, Ehrman Mitchell, George Notter, Gregory Palmero, Ted Pappas, I.M. Pei, Cesar Pelli, Thom Penney, Skipper Post, Harry Robinson, Jim Scheeler, Chuck Schwing, Larry Segrue, Bill Slayton, Chris Smith, Bob Stern, Dean Cecil Steward, Hugh Stubbins, Tom Teasdale, Randy Vosbeck, Chet Widom, Henry Wright, and so many more. Thank you to the AIA Gold Medallists for permission to quote from their acceptance speeches and to the AIA Archives for its research assistance.

This book would not have been possible without the constant support of family and friends who offered ideas and were my best critics in the early drafts. Special thanks go to my mother Carol Cramer, wife Corinne Cramer, sons Austin Cramer and Ryan Cramer, as well as to Weld Coxe, Arthur Gensler, John Hoke, and Earl Powell. Linda Ebitz, Tina Kennedy, Pam Kortan, B.J. Musselman, and Janet Rumbarger provided logistical and technical support.

My editor, Ray Rhinehart, Ph.D, vice president of The American Architectural Foundation, is one of the best communicators in America today. He greatly improved my original text and gently guided me forward with decisive wisdom and infectious humor.

Bret Witter, Jennifer Evans Yankopolus, and Mary Pereboom of Greenway edited the revised and updated edition, Austin Cramer created the design and layout was done by Jennie Monahan. Many thanks to these wonderful colleagues.

The team I have worked with has been absolutely incredible! If you like this book, give them the credit. If you don't, the fault is mine. This is certain: There is much experience and insight possessed by those I have been fortunate to work with. What impresses me most is what they are continuing to do with what they have.

They have a strong vision of a better way—of a new reality in architecture.

—James P. Cramer, Hon. AIA, Hon. IIDA, CAE

James P. Cramer is Chairman of The Greenway Group, a design management consulting firm headquartered in Atlanta, Georgia. He is also adjunct professor of architecture at the University of Hawaii, Manoa.

The Greenway Group was founded in 1982 to significantly increase the performance and capability of A/E/C and design industry organizations. Greenway consults worldwide on ownership transitions, corporate repositioning, strategic planning, organizational design, and marketing and branding. It is also well known for its executive search expertise.

The former CEO of The American Institute of Architects and publisher of *Architecture* magazine, Jim Cramer is the co-chair of the Design Futures Council, a think-tank that brings together industry leaders to anticipate and take advantage of futures trends and innovations. He is also editor of the monthly newsletter, *DesignIntelligence*, a leader in sharing trends, strategies and forecasts related to futures innovation for the design professions and the entire A/E/C industry.

A prominent speaker, writer, and researcher, Cramer is a frequent lecturer at major events. He gives seminars for design firms, developers and product manufacturers, and his public seminars are attended by thousands of designers each year. He is the founder of Greenway Communications, and the co-editor of the critically-acclaimed *Almanac of Architecture & Design*.

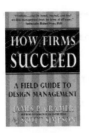

ORDER FORM

How Firms Succeed: A Field Guide to Design Management: $39

Design plus Enterprise: $29

Almanac of Architecture & Design: $37.50

DesignIntelligence (including a one-year membership to the Design Futures Council): $228 annually

Shipping: $4.95
(add $1.50 per additional title)

NOTE: Shipping is included with DesignIntelligence—there is NO additional charge

Title	Quantity	Price:
	Shipping	

❑ Check   ❑ Credit card   Order Total

Card #   Expiration   Signature

Contact/Shipping Information

Name   Company

Address

City   State   Zip

Telephone   Fax

Email

Please fax this form to Greenway Communications: (770) 209-3778 or mail: Greenway Communications, 30 Technology Parkway South, Suite 200, Norcross, GA 30092. For additional information call (800) 726-8603.

östberg ™

Library of Design Management

Every relationship of value requires constant care and commitment. At Östberg, we are relentless in our desire to create and bring forward only the best ideas in design, architecture, interiors, and design management. Using diverse mediums of communications, including books and the Internet, we are constantly searching for thoughtful ideas that are erudite, witty, and of lasting importance to the quality of life. Inspired by the architecture of Ragnar Östberg and the best of Scandinavian design and civility, the Östberg Library of Design Management seeks to restore the passion for creativity that makes better products, spaces, and communities. The essence of Östberg can be summed up in our quality charter to you: "Communicating concepts of leadership and design excellence."